GREAT WOMEN IN
AMERICAN HISTORY

GREAT WOMEN IN AMERICAN HISTORY

by

Rebecca Price Janney
III

HORIZON BOOKS
CAMP HILL, PENNSYLVANIA

Horizon Books
3825 Hartzdale Drive, Camp Hill, PA 17011

Faithful, biblical publishing since 1883

ISBN: 0-88965-130-2
© 1996 by Horizon Books

98 99 00 01 02   6 5 4 3 2

Illustrations by Karl Foster

DEDICATION

To the memory of Catherine Marshall, a great woman who showed me the Father's love.

CONTENTS

ACKNOWLEDGMENTS

————⊃※⊂————

A book like this can come about only with a lot of assistance, from professional researchers to family and friends. Thank you, Karen Knapp, for supplying many names of great American women for consideration. I am also grateful to the following libraries for aiding me with my considerable research—the Abington Free Library, Biblical Theological Seminary Library, where Joanna Hause helped me, the Learning Resource Center at Philadelphia College of the Bible, Lourdes Library at Gwynedd-Mercy College and Myrin Library at Ursinus College, particularly for David's expert advice and eagerness to help. I also drew invaluable foundational material for many of my biographies from Robert McHenry's book, *Famous American Women*.

My friends Michael Fletcher, Neil Babcox and Robert Austell provided much-appreciated advice and material for this book. My editor,

David Fessenden, was always there when I needed him and gave me a very long leash; I deeply appreciate his counsel as well as his sensitivity. And finally, I want to thank my husband, Scott, for his unfailing encouragement and incredible patience with me whenever I "go out to sea" with a new book. You're the best!

INTRODUCTION

———✦———

I just spent several weeks in the company of some incredible women from America's past. Most of the twenty-three ladies you are about to meet sent me from my research with a spring in my step and a renewed determination to fulfill all that God has planned for me.

These women's lives cross racial, religious, educational and socio-economic lines. They also stretch the length and width of American history, from Pocahontas in the opening years of the seventeenth century, to Rosa Parks in the closing ones of the twentieth. In addition, they represent many walks of life: first ladies, religious leaders, educators, patriots, social activists, true-to-life heroines, writers, a businesswoman and a singer. You will recognize many of their names immediately, while others will be much less familiar.

What is the common thread that binds these disparate women together? What can an aristocratic first lady possibly share with a runaway slave or a stately queen with a "hallelujah lassie"? And why write a book like this in the first place?

Each of these women was chosen as *a person of faith and principle*. Many, like Frances Willard and Eliza Shirley, made a mark on history by expressing their faith; others, like Rosa Parks and Martha Washington, exercised faith as they saw history being made all around them. Yet for all these *Great Women in American History*, faith in God formed the cornerstone of their lives.

Furthermore, this book is necessary for three major reasons:

1. It provides a compelling introduction to these women's lives, a brief encounter that may lead you to a lengthier acquaintance.

2. It also portrays them as flesh-and-blood people with foibles and faults like everyone else, who through faith in God, fulfilled the mighty purposes for which He made each one. This is the approach the Bible takes in its portrayal of faith's heroes. It has not been a common approach in studying figures from American history, however. Before about 1970, biographies tended to paint these women's lives in an idealized way, holding them up as people who could do no wrong. After that, however, historians began smashing the "idols" of our past, telling us how base and cunning they really were, leaving many to wonder what was so great about them anyway. *Great Women*

in American History is neither naive nor icono-
clastic; I have ventured to present an accurate
picture of courageous women of faith and principle whose deeds should not be downplayed
because of their clay feet, or vice-versa.

3. Lastly, this book, like many written longer
than twenty-five years ago, gives faith its right-
ful place in American history. I am dismayed
that so many contemporary biographical ac-
counts of heroic women of faith omit any reference to God, or cast their faith in a negative
light. How many children, for instance, who
saw Disney's *Pocahontas* know that she became
a dynamic Christian woman?

You may wonder why all but one of these biographies are about dead women, why I have
not chosen to write about today's great female
figures. It is primarily because their lives have
not reached the fullness of time, that point at
which their whole story may be told, and perspective can be gained. I will leave that task to
another who will come in twenty-five, fifty or a
hundred years, when the great women of today
will join those of yesterday in having fought the
good fight of our Lord and Savior, Jesus
Christ—unless, of course, He returns by then!

May these stories prompt you to live fully
and beautifully for Him.

Rebecca Price Janney
May 28, 1996

A BIGAIL
A DAMS

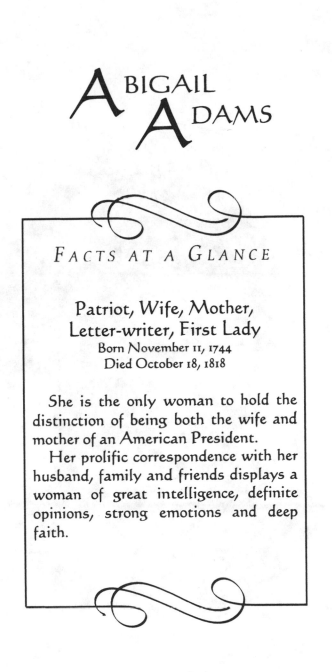

FACTS AT A GLANCE

**Patriot, Wife, Mother,
Letter-writer, First Lady**
Born November 11, 1744
Died October 18, 1818

She is the only woman to hold the distinction of being both the wife and mother of an American President.

Her prolific correspondence with her husband, family and friends displays a woman of great intelligence, definite opinions, strong emotions and deep faith.

ABIGAIL ADAMS

Shortly after Abigail Smith and John Adams were married in 1764, they separated—not by conflict, but by necessity. To supplement the meager income from their farm and provide for their growing family, John took to the road as an itinerant lawyer. Although neither he nor Abigail was happy about the frequent separations, they endured them in order to make it financially.

Once Adams had distinguished himself and was ready to stop traveling so much, another duty called him back on the road. He and Abigail became ardent patriots in the American cause against Great Britain. In 1774 Adams became a representative to the First Continental Congress in Philadelphia. Shortly after her husband's new appointment, Abigail wrote to a friend, "I find I am obliged to summon all my patriotism to feel willing to part with him again. You will readily believe me when I say that I make no small sacrifice to the public."[1]

John Adams became indispensable to the fortunes of the new country during the Revolution (1776-1781), and this meant constant travel. In November 1777 Congress appointed him commissioner to the court of France. His absence left a "Craveing void" for his wife.[2] About a year later, her husband became Minister Plenipotentiary to Great Britain.

Abigail had full responsibility for their farm and household, including handling finances, raising their four children and caring for elderly parents and sick relatives. Sometimes, as in 1777 when she endured the death of her stillborn child alone, her husband's absence was wrenching.

Not until 1784 did she get to join him in Europe. As he eagerly awaited her arrival, Adams told a newlywed colleague, "I hope to be married once more myself, in a few months, to a very amiable lady whom I have inhumanly left a widow in America for nine years, with the exception of a few weeks only."[3]

Someone asked Abigail in her twilight years if she regretted all the separations between her and her "dearest Friend." She responded:

I feel a pleasure in being able to sacrifice my selfish passions to the general good, and in imitating the example which has taught me to consider myself and family but as the small dust of the balance, when compared with the great community.[4]

John Milton's famous words could have been written with her in mind: "They also serve who stand and wait."

Born in Weymouth, Massachusetts in 1744, Abigail Smith came from a distinguished family that had been in America for five generations. Abigail was the second of Elizabeth Quincy and William Smith's four children. Her father was a Congregational minister who raised his children to be completely devoted to Christ and family.

Abigail, a frail child, yearned to go beyond the basic subjects for colonial girls—math, reading, music, dancing and needlework. While she liked those disciplines, Abigail was an insatiable reader who loved Milton and Shakespeare, Pope and Thomson. She had no formal education, yet she became fluent in French and had a vigorous mind.

She met John Adams in 1758, but they did not pursue a relationship until four years later. Initially Adams had been dubious of the Reverend Smith who, in his opinion, lived too high for a minister. On the other hand, Smith con-

sidered Adams as too low-born for his daughter. At any rate, John Adams was nine years
Abigail's senior, already a Harvard graduate
and lawyer.

In 1762 they were reintroduced with better
results and were married on October 25, 1764.
The Adamses had five children in ten years and
enjoyed each other enormously throughout
their fifty-four-year marriage. Historian Paul F.
Boller, Jr. said theirs "was one of America's
great love stories."[5]

Abigail was a willing student and John a willing teacher of farming, law, politics and religion. Regarding the latter, they preferred
simple expressions of faith; too much adorn-
ment made them uneasy. To them the important thing was to have a vital, obedient faith,
one that carried them through all their joys and
heartaches.

From 1774-1784 the Adamses were apart
more than together because of John's political
activities in Philadelphia and abroad, and
Abigail wrote to her husband prodigiously. He
kept pace with her considerable output until
his politically delicate tenure in Europe. His
letters were often lost at sea on their way to
America. In addition, John held back a lot in
his expressions of affection, as well as his political news, afraid that either he or Abigail's
missives might be intercepted and used publicly to embarrass him or the U.S. Those were
the darkest months for Abigail, who couldn't

bear not to hear from him regularly and uncensored.

In 1781 he wrote to her from Holland:

> What a fine Affair it would be if We could flit across the Atlantic as they say Angels do from Planet to Planet. I would dart to Penns Hill and bring you over on my Wings.[6]

Her letters dealt with family, friends and the doings of the farm, as well as her meditations on the times in which they lived. According to Robert McHenry, "they provide a sprightly and fascinating view of life in those trying times."[7]

Abigail Adams was every inch the patriot, like her husband. Central to that fervor was her Christian faith. Only righteousness, she maintained, could exalt a nation. Her faith also prepared her to make the greatest sacrifice, if necessary:

> If the Sword be drawn I bid adieu to all domestick felicity, and look forward to the Country where there is neither wars nor rumors of War in a firm belief that thro the mercy of its King we shall both rejoice there together.[8]

The only certainty in life, she constantly told her children, was God. Their commitment to

Him must come before all other things. She wrote to them:

> Improve your understanding for acquiring useful knowledge and virtue, such as will render you an ornament to society, an Honour to your Country and a Blessing to your parents. Great Learning and superior abilities, should you ever possess them, will be of little value and small Estimation, unless Virtue, Honour, Truth and integrity are added to them. Adhere to those religious Sentiments and principals which are early instilled into your mind and remember that you are accountable to your Maker for all your words and actions. Let me injoin it upon you to attend constantly and steadfastly to the precepts and instructions of your Father as you value the happiness of your Mother and your own welfare. . . . I had much rather you should have found your Grave in the ocean you have crossd or any untimely death crop you in your Infant years, rather than see you an immoral profligate or a Graceless child.[9]

Abigail was blissfully reunited with her husband in Paris in 1784. One thing she did not find to her liking, however, was France's festival atmosphere on Sundays. She also complained when the American government wouldn't allow its embassy to have chaplains. Abigail openly wondered whether America's political ministers weren't in need of grace. During that time she worshiped at the Dutch ambassador's chapel.

The following year, John Adams became the United States' first minister to Great Britain, and Abigail accompanied him to London. Upon their return to the United States, Adams pursued a political career with Abigail's enthusiastic support. Largely due to her unselfishness, America did not lose the formidable talents of one of its most auspicious Founding Fathers.

The couple resided in the country's first capitols, New York, Philadelphia and Washington, when John became vice-president under George Washington and later President. Abigail Adams became the first presidential wife to live in the White House, which remained unfinished during her husband's term. She hosted many official dinners, which guests found stimulating largely due to her lively conversation.

President Adams depended on his wife to read and comment on his speeches, as well as to discuss events and policies with him. She was his "sounding board," the one person he most trusted.[10] Abigail also had a way of making sure that newspaper editors received good news about him to print.

Mrs. Adams had strong views about the role of women in public life. She believed that women should be better educated and have more legal autonomy, but maintained that domestic life was best for them. A good wife and mother, she felt, could serve her country in those capacities. Curiously, she is presently the only woman to have had both a husband and son (John Quincy Adams) in the White House.

In the election of 1800 she judged the candidates running against her husband on the basis of their religious beliefs. For example, she considered Thomas Jefferson, whom she greatly admired, to be barely Christian because he didn't believe in a God active in the world's affairs. On the other hand, she felt that despite vice-presidential candidate Aaron Burr's orthodox beliefs, he had more to answer to God for because of his arrogance and hot temper.

Following John Adams' defeat by Thomas Jefferson, the Adamses retired to their home in Braintree, Massachusetts. They became "gentlemen farmers," finally enjoying the togetherness for which they had longed.

Abigail Adams's health began to deteriorate around the time of her daughter Nabby's death in 1814. Nevertheless, she retained a cheerful outlook, sustained by her faith and the belief that "the laughing philosopher (is) a much wiser man than the sniveling one."[11] She contracted typhoid fever in October 1818 and died on the 18th, a few weeks before her seventy-fourth birthday. The first volume of her letters appeared in print in 1840, published by her grandson, Charles Francis Adams.

Endnotes

1. Levin Phyllis Lee. *Abigail Adams: A Biography* (New York: St. Martin's Press, 1987), p. 50.
2. Ibid., p. 104.
3. Ibid., p. 148.
4. Boller, Paul F., Jr. *Presidential Wives: An Anecdotal History* (New York: Oxford University Press, 1988), p. 13.
5. Ibid., p. 15.
6. Ibid.,
7. NMcHenry, Robert, ed. *Famous American Women* (New York: Dover Publications, 1980), p. 2.
8. Ibid.
9. Levin, pp. 119-120.
10. Boller, p. 19.
11. Ibid., p. 20.

Marian Anderson

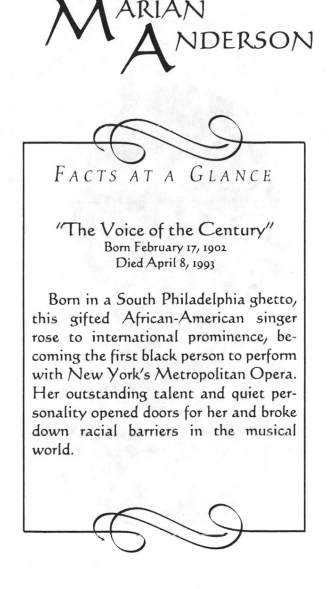

Facts at a Glance

"The Voice of the Century"
Born February 17, 1902
Died April 8, 1993

Born in a South Philadelphia ghetto, this gifted African-American singer rose to international prominence, becoming the first black person to perform with New York's Metropolitan Opera. Her outstanding talent and quiet personality opened doors for her and broke down racial barriers in the musical world.

MARIAN ANDERSON

A dense fog enveloped the plane carrying singer Marian Anderson and her accompanist, Kosti Vehanen. The two passengers began to worry. In the 1930s Marian had become a European singing sensation, particularly in the Scandinavian countries. Now she found herself on a flight from Stockholm, Sweden to Helsinki, Finland in miserable weather, with visibility at near zero.

"We should have landed in Helsinki five minutes ago," Marian said, anxiously glancing at her watch.

"I know," Kosti replied. He could see inside the cockpit where the pilots were frantically trying to figure out their exact location. Just then the motor slowed and the plane began its descent.

"How can they see through the fog?" Marian worried aloud.

"I—" Kosti's response was cut off with a gasp as a radio tower suddenly appeared out of nowhere. The plane was heading straight toward it!

Marian closed her eyes, not so much to avoid the sight as to pray. With clasped hands she implored God's help. The plane swerved sharply, missing the tower by inches. It scraped against treetops as the pilot struggled to avoid crashing. Shortly afterward, the vehicle landed safely.

Marian and her companion hurried off the plane, eager to be on steady ground again. They saw a man run toward them. Kosti whispered, "The mayor of Helsinki."

"Miss Anderson! Mr. Vehanen!" he cried. "I want to congratulate you on your safe arrival."

"Thank you, Mr. Mayor," Marian answered graciously.

"Perhaps we should all be thanking Marian for the safe landing," said Kosti. "I'm sure she prayed for it."

"I imagine everyone on the plane was praying," she replied.

"They probably were," Kosti answered. "But somehow I have the feeling that Marian Anderson's voice is heard before anyone else's!"[1]

Born in an integrated South Philadelphia neighborhood in 1902, Marian Anderson showed an early flair for singing. Her parents, however, could not afford formal lessons. John Anderson sold ice and coal at the Reading Terminal Market, while his wife Anna cleaned houses and took in laundry. She had been a school teacher in Virginia but could not find such a position in Philadelphia.

From the age of six Marian sang in the Union Baptist Church choir, where she performed bass, alto, tenor *and* soprano parts, earning her the nickname "Baby Contralto." As word of her talent spread, churches all over the city began asking her to sing. Her father encouraged Marian to develop her truly stunning voice range and bought her a piano with his hard-earned savings.

When Marian was just ten, her father died of a brain tumor and money got tighter than ever. Anna Anderson took Marian and her two other daughters to live with their father's parents to save money. The house was crowded enough as it was; the elder Andersons had already taken in their own daughter and her children.

Marian's financial need did not go unnoticed, however. The members of Union Baptist Church, led by choir master Alexander Robinson, raised enough funds for the prodigy to attend a year of music school when she was seventeen. However, when Marian tried to register at a Philadelphia academy, she was turned away because of her color. Anna Anderson refused to raise a fuss about the incident, telling Marian that something else would work out.

According to biographer Shirlee P. Newman, "No matter how many times she was offended for the fact she was a Negro, Marian Anderson rose above ignorance. She held her head high, wore her color proudly."[2] Her feeling was, "The Lord isn't prejudiced. He gave this gift (of singing) to a Negro."[3]

Roland Hayes, the famous black tenor, offered to take Marian to Boston where she could study under his voice teacher. By working for the man's wife as a housekeeper, Marian could earn her lessons. It seemed like an ideal proposal, but the young singer's grandmother would not allow it. It wasn't proper, Grandmother Anderson contended, for young girls to go off like that by themselves.

Instead Marian continued performing throughout Philadelphia, making a few dollars here and there. She also joined the city's black Choral Society. During her junior year in high school, Miss Anderson began studying voice under Mary Patterson, a black woman so taken with the youngster's talent that she offered free lessons. That arrangement lasted for only a few months, at which time Patterson told the gifted teenager she had nothing more to teach her. Instead she sent Marian to contralto Agnes Reifsnyder with funds raised by a Philadelphia Choral Society benefit concert.

Shortly afterward a student of famed voice instructor Giuseppe Boghetti introduced Marian to the maestro. "I am tired," he told her bluntly when they met. "I have more pupils than I need already. Make no mistake. I listen to you only as a favor to Miss Roma. Understand?"[4] He impatiently looked at Marian's music, "Deep River," grumbling that he'd never heard it. By the time she finished singing, however, Marian had won over the crusty teacher. "I will make room for you at once," he stated enthusiastically. "I will need only two years with you. After that, you will be able to go anywhere, sing for anybody."[5]

Many years later that Boghetti recalled that audition. "When she finished singing 'Deep River,' I just couldn't move. She had none of the refinements. She simply sang it the way she felt it, with all her natural feeling for music."[6]

Paying for lessons from Boghetti intimidated the young singer, but her church came through again, raising over $600. In spite of Boghetti's zeal for her talent, however, he discouraged Marian about an operatic career. He directed her toward the concert stage, knowing there was no room for a black person in opera.

When she wasn't practicing, Marian performed frequently in churches, clubs, halls, schools and private parties, earning a fairly good income. One performance in Virginia was attended by the famed black composer/musician R. Nathaniel Dett. "You'll have many sacrifices to make," Dett told her afterward in the tone of one artist counseling another. "But even if your dreams never come true, the effort in itself is worthwhile."[7]

One of those sacrifices came when Orpheus "King" Fisher, an architectural and art student in Philadelphia, proposed marriage. Marian was deeply fond of him, but she did not want marriage to interfere with her career, or her career to interfere with her marriage. He said that he would wait. As in all her life's decisions, faith sustained her. One of her favorite songs was, "He's Got the Whole World in His Hands." It was, she remarked, "more, much more, than a number on a concert program. This song reminds us not to lose sight of the fact that we have our times of extremity and that there is a Being who can help us at such a time."[8]

At the age of twenty-three Marian was chosen over 300 other candidates in a major competition at New York's Lewisohn Stadium. As her prize, she had the privilege to sing with the New York Philharmonic Orchestra. Social realities tempered the positive reviews of her performance on August 26, 1925: "She has a beautiful voice," said the papers. "Too bad she's a Negro."

She continued to sing in small venues, waiting for a big break to take her past obscurity to greater opportunities. But they never came. Marian and Boghetti agreed that Europe offered the best chance for her to make it big.

In 1930 she made her continental debut in Berlin, followed by tours throughout Europe during the early 1930s, all of them successful. She also sang for royalty in England, Sweden, Norway and Denmark. The Finnish composer Sibelius was so taken with her that he wrote "Solitude" as a tribute to Miss Anderson.

In the process of becoming a star in Europe's concert halls, Marian Anderson also turned into a sophisticated and beautiful woman whose style European women copied. But the singer's feet remained firmly planted; she never thought more highly of herself than was right or abandoned the simple, childlike faith she had embraced in Philadelphia. This was evidenced during her first airplane ride from Stockholm to Helsinki.

As the plane ascended, Marian caught her breath at the sight of a gorgeous rainbow set against the clouds. She told her accompanist, Kosti Vehanen, "Now I understand. If the good Lord doesn't like to behold the misery on earth, He covers it from His sight with clouds. But where there are human beings, there is always a dark shadow." Kosti smiled at her, knowing that for all her sophistication, "she would always remain the same religious girl who had sung in the choir at church."[9]

About that time Marian wrote to her mother asking what one special thing she could buy for her, something Anna Anderson had always wanted but never could afford. Marian was now in a position to grant her mother's wish. Mrs. Anderson wrote back to say that all she wanted "was that God . . . would hold (you) in the hollow of His hand."[10]

Marian got to visit the atheistic Soviet Union during her tour of Europe, and officials told her not to perform anything "religious." Nevertheless, she sang about the hope of God in their concert halls, once with Joseph Stalin in attendance. She said bluntly, "They are the songs of my people. I shall sing them whenever and wherever I please."[11] After her first recital in the USSR, people rushed to the stage and pounded on it, shouting, " 'Deep River!' 'Heaven, Heaven!' "[12] She gave them their encore.

Her first American performance in several years took place in December 1935 at Town Hall in New York. It was as triumphant as her first New York performance (in 1924) had been dismal, when a tiny audience did not hear the discouraged young singer at her best. The 1935 audience was much more appreciative, and afterward the famous conductor Arturo Toscanini proclaimed that a voice like hers was heard only once in a century.

Although Miss Anderson had been restricted from appearing in many of America's largest musical arenas because of her race, she did not complain about the situation. She preferred to let her singing speak for her, to use it to help others overcome prejudice. In the most trying racial incident she ever encountered, she also discovered she had many friends who came to her defense.

It began in mid-1938 when Howard University in Washington, D.C. invited her to sing. Constitution Hall, owned by the Daughters of the American Revolution (DAR), was the only place in the city large enough to accommodate the expected crowds. But when Miss Anderson's agent, Sol Hurok, tried to make reservations for the April 9, 1939 concert, he was informed that the hall was reserved for that date. Hurok submitted other dates, but all were turned down. Finally he asked another concert master to request the same dates, and found that every one was available. It became obvious that Negroes were not welcome at Constitution Hall.

Shock waves pulsed through the music world, and several well-known artists canceled their appearances at the Hall. Violinist Jascha Heifetz remarked, "I am ashamed to play at Constitution Hall."[13] First Lady Eleanor Roosevelt publicly revoked her membership from the DAR in her newspaper column, "My Day," creating a major sensation. Other prominent women quit the DAR as well, and several local chapters lodged protests.

The United States Department of the Interior offered to let Miss Anderson sing at an outdoor concert at the Lincoln Memorial on Easter Sunday. She reluctantly agreed. The affair had upset her, but like it or not, said Hurok, she had become a symbol of her race.[14] She appeared that day, nervous and determined as Secretary of the Interior Harold Ickes introduced her to the audience of 75,000.

Her voice rose like a benediction over her enraptured listeners in song after song. When the concert ended, the crisp spring air reverberated with stormy applause. Miss Anderson stepped to the microphone saying, "I am overwhelmed. I can't tell you what you have done for me today. I thank you from the bottom of my heart again and again."[15] Kosti Vehanen remarked, "God in His great wisdom opened the door to His most beautiful cathedral . . . that glorious Easter Sunday."[16]

Four years later in 1943 Secretary Ickes unveiled a mural of the event at the Department of the Interior. He said, "Marian Anderson's voice and personality have come to be a symbol of the willing acceptance of the immortal truth that 'all men are created equal.' "[17] The following day she sang at Constitution Hall at the request of the DAR at a war benefit for China Relief.

Eleanor Roosevelt presented Marian with the Spingarn Medal from the National Association for the Advancement of Colored People, the First Lady noting that the singer had not changed her dignified or warm manner in the least since her American star had risen. In 1941 Miss Anderson also received Philadelphia's Bok Award, given to the citizen of which the city is most proud.

In spite of the awards and praise, however, Marian Anderson continued to endure embarrassing, mind-numbing prejudice, like the time she received the key to Atlantic City, New Jersey, and was refused a room in a hotel there. Or when she sang at the premier of a film on Abraham Lincoln in Illinois, and was declined lodging at the Lincoln Hotel.[18] Still, she persisted with dignity and warmth.

Orpheus "King" Fisher, the architect who had proposed more than a decade earlier, had persisted in waiting for her. They finally got married in July 1943 and bought a home on a farm in Danbury, Connecticut. At forty-one Marian loved her new adventure as a wife. "Marriage to King was worth waiting for," she remarked happily.[19]

Five years later a cyst on her throat posed a grave threat to Marian's career. Specialists insisted on surgery, but they could not promise she ever would sing again. Such a procedure could result in permanent injury to the vocal chords. She went through with it anyway, saying the Lord had given her that voice to begin with, and it was up to Him whether she should keep it or not.[20] A month after the surgery, she was singing again.

In the fall of 1954 she became the first black to sing with New York's Metropolitan Opera. She took the role of Ulrica, the black sorceress in Verdi's "The Masked Ball." *The New York Times* welcomed the opportunity to hear her in this medium adding, "When there has been discrimination against Marian Anderson, the suffering was not hers, but ours. It was we who were impoverished, not she."[21]

During the dress rehearsal, she answered many questions from reporters, often using "we" and "one" instead of "I" when talking about herself. When they asked her why she did so she responded:

> Because the longer one lives, the surer one is that the "I" in it is very small. There is nothing one has done alone. The composers, the people who make the pianos, the accompanist, the Lord who gives us the breath, make possible anything one does.[22]

On opening night, she received a standing ovation *before* she started to sing. Well-wishers and journalists mobbed her dressing room afterward. When they all had gone, Anna Anderson kissed her daughter. "We thank the Lord," she said simply, putting the event in proper perspective.[23]

Two years later Miss Anderson toured twelve countries for the Department of State besides her singing engagements. The government sent her because of Marian's understanding nature and the way she related to all kinds of people. At Ewha Women's University in Seoul, South Korea, she received an honorary doctorate. University President Helen Kim said, "You are respected as a leader among women. Your success against great odds has encouraged others in their struggle for justice and human rights. You stand as an example of Christian service to mankind."[24]

She also kept busy writing her autobiography, *My Lord, What a Morning*, which was published in 1956. The next year President Eisenhower invited Miss Anderson to sing the national anthem at his second inaugural, then appointed her a member of the U.S. delegation to the United Nations. Her appeal easily crossed party lines. When Democrat John F. Kennedy was inaugurated on January 21, 1961, she also sang the national anthem for him. The Kennedys frequently invited her to perform at the White House, and JFK decided to present Miss Anderson with the Presidential Medal of Freedom. He was assassinated a few weeks before the ceremony, however, and President Lyndon Johnson gave her the award instead on December 6, 1963.

Marian Anderson was growing older as she had done everything else, gracefully. Now in her sixties, she did her American and European farewell tours in 1964-65. She remained active in the Freedom from Hunger Fund, which she had helped create to eliminate world famine, as well as other charitable causes. When she turned seventy-five, a concert in her honor took place at Carnegie Hall in New York. First Lady Rosalyn Carter delivered a Congressional resolution of congratulations, and the city of

New York presented Miss Anderson with its Handel Medallion.

About that time her husband suffered a crippling stroke, and Marian lovingly nursed him. He died in 1986; they had been married for forty-three years. Her faith helped her cope with that loss, as it had assisted her through all the indignities and trials she had endured throughout her life. She said, "When things happen along the way which might pull one up rather sharply, through disappointment think on your faith and go back."[25]

Someone asked Marian Anderson to look back over her long and illustrious career and recall what had been the happiest day of her life. She replied, "The happiest day in my life was when I told my mother she didn't need to work anymore."[26]

Miss Anderson died on April 8, 1993 at age ninety-one. The voice of the century had been silenced.

Endnotes

1. Newman, Shirlee P. *Marian Anderson: Lady from Philadelphia* (Philadelphia: Westminster Press, 1966), pp. 75-76.
2. Ibid., p. 32.
3. Ibid., p. 39.
4. Ibid., p. 25.
5. Ibid., p. 26.
6. Ibid., p. 27.
7. Ibid, pp. 31-32.

8. Tedards, Anne. *Marian Anderson* (New York: Chelsea House Publishers, 1988), p. 83.
9. Newman, p. 75.
10. Ibid., p. 76.
11. Ibid., p. 79.
12. Ibid., p. 79.
13. Ibid., p. 105.
14. Ibid., p. 107.
15. Ibid., p. 110.
16. Ferris, Jeri. *The Story of Marian Anderson* (Minneapolis: Carolrhoda Books, Inc., 1994), p. 74.
17. Newman, p. 111.
18. Ferris, p. 79.
19. Newman, p. 116.
20. Ibid., p. 129.
21. Ibid., p. 134.
22. Ibid., p. 135.
23. Ibid., p. 136.
24. Ibid., pp. 141-42.
25. Tedards, p. 101.
26. Newman, p. 154.

Mary McLeod Bethune

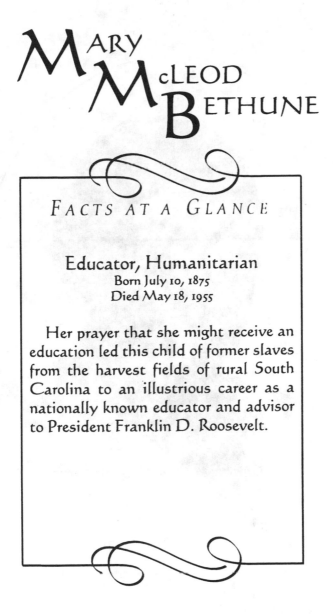

FACTS AT A GLANCE

Educator, Humanitarian
Born July 10, 1875
Died May 18, 1955

Her prayer that she might receive an education led this child of former slaves from the harvest fields of rural South Carolina to an illustrious career as a nationally known educator and advisor to President Franklin D. Roosevelt.

MARY McLEOD BETHUNE

Patsy McLeod lugged a basket of freshly washed and ironed clothes to her former master Ben Wilson's house. Her nine-year-old daughter Mary tagged along, happy to have a morning off from pulling weeds in their cotton field. When they arrived at the big house, the McLeods walked past the front entrance to the rear one used for blacks. In 1884 there was sharp segregation between the races in Mayesville, South Carolina.

While her mother went inside for the few cents that doing the Wilsons' clothes brought in, Mary wandered over to a magical-looking children's playhouse and peeked inside. Two white girls about her age sat among an impressive collection of dolls, scaled-down furniture and lovely china dishes.

"Hello, Mary! Do you want to come in?" one of them called out.

Of course she did. Mary wasn't admitted to such circles every day.

"Let's play we're keeping house," the white child decided. "You can watch the baby while I have tea with my friend." She shoved a doll at the black girl.

Mary held the beautiful object to her breast, then gave a start when her white peer scolded her for not making the "baby" stop crying. "It's spoiling my tea," the girl complained.

Mary got up and walked the doll around the room. Suddenly her eyes fell upon a book; she picked it up in awe. Her parents had a Bible in their cabin, but no one could read it. To have another book just lying around casually was beyond her comprehension. Unexpectedly the white girl swooped down upon her and grabbed the book. "Put that down!" she yelled. "*You* don't know how to read."

Mary tingled with shame as she handed the doll back to her hostess and rejoined her mother. On the walk back to their farm, she wondered why white people were so different from black people, why they had all kinds of nice things and got to boss everybody around and why, above all, they could read while black people were kept in ignorance. Did the inequality have something to do with reading and education?

Deciding that was the case, Mary prayed, "Dear Lord, I don't think we're so free. Help me to get educated." She decided then and there, "I'm going to learn to read. I'm going to learn to read!" At home the little girl asked her father's permission to go to school, but he told her somberly, "There isn't any school."

One day, however, a black woman in city clothes changed that. Miss Emma Wilson came to the McLeod cabin explaining that the Mission Board of the Presbyterian Church had sent her to get a school going in Mayesville for black children. "The school will begin after the cotton-picking season," she emphasized, hoping to attract as many young scholars as she could.

Sam and Patsy McLeod looked at each other, then smiled in agreement. "We can spare this one," Mrs. McLeod told the woman, nodding toward her daughter.

Young Mary was beside herself. "I'm gonna read? You mean I'm gonna read, Miss Wilson?" As the woman smiled tenderly, the little girl murmured, "Thank you, Ma'am." Then she sank to her knees and folded her hands. "Thank You, God, for delivering me."[1]

Samuel and Patsy McLeod were former slaves who had a cotton farm near Mayesville, South Carolina. They also had seventeen children. Mary Jane, born ten years after the Civil War, was the fifteenth. Most of the oldest ones were married and settled in other cabins by the time Mary reached adolescence, and while the first children had been born into slavery, Mary and her two younger siblings were born free.

"Grandmother Sophia" was part of the family, too, sitting in the living room smoking a pipe while the others worked the farm. Sophia had lived in slavery most of her life, working hard for her master. Therefore her children exempted her from helping out, saying that Sophia had earned a good, long rest. Mary McLeod often overheard her grandmother pray, "Dear God, I am so happy to be living in this loving family, where I can get hot biscuits and butter, and coffee with cream, sitting at my own fireplace."

At night Mary and her family sang hymns and told stories. Mary loved to hear Sophia's tales about life on the plantation, thankful that she didn't have to live in slavery. Just the same, she knew that without an education, most blacks would continue to live in poverty and ignorance.

At age nine Mary McLeod took her first steps toward a better life when she started attending Emma Wilson's school. It was located five miles from home near the Methodist church to which her family belonged. Mayesville Institute started in the living room of an old shack and, like most schools for blacks in the post-Civil War years, arose from the missionary efforts of Northern churches. Every night after dinner, Mary McLeod taught her family what she had learned that day at school. She also started helping neighbors with math problems related to their farming businesses, becoming a celebrated young figure in the community.

Mary graduated from the school at age twelve, but she yearned for further education. Her parents thought they could afford it—until tragedy struck. In the midst of planting cotton, the McLeod's donkey suddenly dropped dead in the field. There would be no money for a new animal until harvest time, so each family member took his or her turn pulling the plow. Mary prayed for another miracle so she could go back to school, but she kept herself from hoping too much.

One sticky summer day, however, Mary spotted her former teacher walking toward her across the field. Emma Wilson had wonderful news. A Quaker woman from Colorado had used her life savings to provide a scholarship for a black child to go to Scotia Seminary in Concord, North Carolina (a secondary school) and Mary was to be the recipient. Years later she recalled that miraculous day:

Oh, the joy of that glorious morning! I can never forget it. To this day my heart thrills with gratitude at the memory of that day. I was but a little girl, groping for the light, dreaming dreams and seeing visions in the cotton and rice fields, and away off in Denver, Colorado, a poor dressmaker, sewing for her daily bread, heard my call and came to my assistance. Out of her scanty earnings she invested in a life—my life!—And while God gives me strength, I shall strive to pass on to others the opportunities that this noble woman toiled and sacrificed to give me. How many self-denials she must have made! How many little legitimate pleasures she must have foregone, that the little black girl in South Carolina might have a chance.[2]

At Scotia both black and white teachers conducted Mary McLeod's classes, and she learned that not all whites wanted to keep blacks down. (The school, founded in 1867 by the Presbyterian Church, is now Barber-Scotia College.) Mary completed the high school course in five years then put in two more years of college-level work, excelling in public speaking and singing. She graduated in 1894.

The young woman applied to Moody Bible Institute so she could become a missionary to Africa. Not only was she accepted, but Mary received another scholarship from her Colorado benefactress, Miss Mary Crissman. Although she was the only black American at the school, there were other people of color, from Africa, Japan, China and India. She recalled:

There we learned to look upon a man as a man, not as a Caucasian or a Negro. My heart had been somewhat hardened. As the whites had meted out to me, I was disposed to measure to them; but here, under this benign influence, including that of Dwight L. Moody, a love for the whole human family, regardless of creed, class, or color, entered my soul . . . .[3]

Besides singing in the choral group, Mary performed for prisoners and handed out gospel literature once a week. She daily served lunch to drunks and street people at the Pacific Garden Mission as well. On one evangelistic trip to the Dakotas, Mary met a five-year-old girl who insisted that she wash before dinner because her skin was so dirty. The child's mother was deeply embarrassed, but Mary just smiled. She held up a vase of flowers saying, "Look at all the different colors of these flowers. God made men just the way he made the flowers, some one color, some another, so that when they are gathered together they make a beautiful bouquet."[4]

In 1895 Mary McLeod graduated from Moody, but the church's mission board said it did not need a black woman to serve in Africa. She described this as "the greatest disappointment of my life."[5] Instead, the twenty-year-old accepted from the board a teaching position at Haines Normal Institute in Augusta, Georgia.

Her supervisor and the school's founder, Lucy Laney, "helped me see," she said later, "that Africans in America need Christ and school just as much as Negroes in Africa."[6]

Following that stint, she went to Kindell Institute in Sumter, near her childhood home. Mary McLeod began to attract many young men, but none of them caught her eye until Albertus Bethune joined her Presbyterian Church choir. He had gone to the Avery Institute in Charleston, South Carolina, but fell shy of a college degree when he quit school to help put his brother through college. Two years later she and Albertus were married at the church parsonage by the Rev. J.C. Watkins.

Albertus got a teaching assignment in Savannah, Georgia, and they rented a small apartment there. Nine months after the birth of their only child, Albert, Mary sensed that the Lord was calling her back to teaching. She took over the mission school in Palatka, Florida, with her husband predicting her early return. Instead, the school thrived under her direction. Realizing that Mary was determined to stay, Albertus went to be with her and their son in Florida.

In 1904 she moved to Florida's Atlantic coast where many blacks were working on the East Coast Railway. She set up a school for their daughters in Daytona Beach, calling it the Daytona Normal and Industrial Institute for Negro Girls. She had no substantial money with which to pursue this course, so Mrs. Bethune worked hard to raise funds for building and equipping the school. Her efforts were particularly rewarded when John D. Rockefeller, Jr. and James N. Gamble of Proctor and Gamble, both vacationers in Florida, took a liking to the spunky teacher. They generously contributed to her school.

The institute, however, grew faster than its funds. Nevertheless, Mary McLeod Bethune's policy was never to turn away a needy child. She remembered where she had come from and was determined that the black children of Daytona should be trained to earn a decent living while dedicating their lives to God.

Albertus found a job driving a taxi and moved into the cottage in which his ambitious wife was living. They regarded the destruction of their home in Palakta by fire as a message to continue on Mary's chosen path with the institute.

When sewing manufacturer Thomas H. White helped build a real school building for them, Mary Bethune hung a sign over the entrance. On the outside it read, "Enter to Learn." And on the inside, "Depart to Serve."

In 1908 the institute admitted some boys and became known as the Daytona Educational Industrial Training School. Mary Bethune's fame spread, and she received an honorary Doctor of Science from Tuskegee Institute, along with the renowned George Washington Carver. (During her life, Bethune received a total of ten honorary degrees.) In 1916 a new building, White Hall, was erected, and at its dedication the vice-president of the United States and the Florida governor made speeches. When Faith Hall was built, Mary Bethune began holding interracial services every Sunday afternoon in its chapel.

Meanwhile young Albert Bethune had been studying at Haines Institute, then went to Morehouse College in Atlanta. He joined the ROTC during the First World War, while his mother traveled about raising funds for the Red Cross. She returned to full-time teaching and administrative duties after the war. Her husband, Albertus, died in 1919.

Mrs. Bethune's school merged with the Cookman Institute for Men in 1923. Six years later it became known as Bethune-Cookman College, and she served as its President until 1942, with another brief interlude in that office from 1946-47, when she finally retired as president emeritus. She resided in a home on the edge of the campus with her secretary, who was on twenty-four-hour call. Mary Bethune remained a zealous fund-raiser who embarked on an ambitious building campaign. She also brought the school to an enrollment of more than 1,000 and to full accreditation, making her nationally famous as an educator.

Mary Bethune was also in demand as a platform speaker, whose addresses about better race relations left listeners with a sense of benediction.[7] She provided a "diplomatic link" between the white and black worlds, striving to gain for her people:

Protection that is guaranteed by the Constitution of the United States and which (the black) has a right to expect; the opportunity for development equal to that of any other American; to be understood; and finally, to make an appreciable contribution to the growth of a better America and a better world.[8]

In 1935 she won the Spingarn Medal of the National Association for the Advancement of Colored People. In response she said, "I never feel worthy of honors, but they are great stimuli to my strength and faith and courage."[9] That year she founded the National Council of Negro Women to improve housing, working conditions, living standards, civil rights and educational opportunities for black women. Although funds for her various projects ran chronically low, Mary always depended on God to come through. When she needed $10,000 to buy a Washington, D.C. house as a headquarters for the Council, she told friends, "I think I shall ask Marshall Field for the money. With God's help, I shall be able to persuade him." They were incredulous, arguing that she didn't even know Field, the Chicago department store magnate. "That's all right,"

Mrs. Bethune countered. "Now, I want the rest of you to start praying; pray all the time I am gone; and don't stop until I get back. Pray that I shall be able to convince Marshall Field that he ought to help me buy the house." She returned from her mission a few hours later with a check for $10,000.[10]

In 1936 President Franklin D. Roosevelt appointed her administrative assistant for Negro affairs of the National Youth Administration (NYA). Her primary function was to obtain part-time jobs for black students affected by the Depression so they could stay in school. She also worked to promote employment for those youths who were not pursuing their educations. At one meeting with FDR she described the economic salvation this program meant for young blacks, bringing the president to tears. Taking her hands in his, he remarked, "Mrs. Bethune, I am glad I am able to contribute something to help make a better life for your people."[12]

She remained with the NYA until 1944, besides advising the secretary of war on the selection of black officer candidates for the new Women's Army Auxiliary Corps. Bethune also assumed the vice-presidency of the NAACP (1940-1955), and when the United Nations held its organizational conference in San Francisco in 1945, she went with the U.S. delegation as an observer. Because she was so active, Bethune's severe asthma was aggravated, and her doctors advised her to slow down. She reluctantly resigned from the presidency of Bethune-Cookman College in 1942 and, after the war, began eliminating some of her federal responsibilities.

In 1950 as she approached retirement, Bethune wrote a foreword to her biography addressing young black people, for whom her heart still burned. She told them:

> Because I see young Mary McLeod in all struggling boys and girls, I can never rest while there is still something that I can do to make the ground firmer under their feet, to make their efforts more productive, to bring their goals nearer, to make their faith in God and their fellow men a little stronger. May those who read this volume . . . gather from it new confidence in themselves, new faith in God, and a willingness to work hard to reach the goals of a good life. Mine has not been an easy road. Very few of my generation found life easy or wanted it that way. . . . I rejoice that in my own way I have been able to demonstrate that there is a place in God's sun for the youth "farthest down" who has the vision, the determination, and the courage to reach it.

Mary McLeod Bethune died of a heart attack on May 18, 1955 in Daytona Beach.

Endnotes

1. Peare, Catherine Owens. *Mary McLeod Bethune* (New York: Vanguard Press, 1951), pp. 27-29, 31, 35.
2. Ibid., p. 49.
3. Ibid., p. 67.
4. Ibid., p. 71.
5. Ibid., p. 73.
6. Ibid., p. 71.
7. Ibid., p. 148.
8. Ibid., p. 153.
9. Ibid., p. 157.
10. Ibid., p. 169.

ANNE BRADSTREET

FACTS AT A GLANCE

America's First Poet
Born 1612
Died September 16, 1672

A highly cultured Puritan who settled in colonial America to escape religious persecution, she began to write poetry to relieve the boredom and hardship of frontier life. When her brother-in-law took her writings to England and had them published, it was the first book of poetry by an American and the first significant one by a British woman.

(The illustration, portaying her in period dress, is an artist's rendition; no portraits are available.)

 Anne Bradstreet

A nne Bradstreet paused from her sweeping and sighed heavily as she took in the crudeness of her surroundings: a house made of rough-hewn wood in a makeshift neighborhood of the same basic dwellings; a tree-dense, rocky countryside that dared farmers to plant crops on it; the absence of paved roads, shops and grand churches to elevate and lighten her sensitive spirit; the presence of native peoples who were sometimes friendly, other times hostile.

It wasn't that Anne disliked adventure or disagreed with her husband and father's reasons for coming to America. She knew that the Puritans needed to get away from constraints put on them by the English government's high-church Anglicans.

The Puritans pursued a more simple faith, void of outward symbols, like special vestments for clergy. Hounded and oppressed by the Anglican government, the Puritans migrated in large numbers to the Massachusetts Bay Colony in pursuit of religious freedom. Anne Bradstreet was among them. The young wife didn't oppose that decision, but adjusting to her new life came with great difficulty. When she first saw the new colony, her heart fell. She wondered how she would ever cope with the crudeness of the frontier.

Raised in the rich culture of Elizabethan England, Anne missed Tattershall Castle and its sculpted English gardens where she was raised. They belonged to the Earl of Lincoln, for whom her father had served as business manager. Nor was there anything in all America like the nobleman's impressive library with its volumes of Shakespeare, Spenser and Johnson swathed in the scent of rich leather.

Not only was there an absence of culture in America, but Anne was frequently ill, as were many others in the strange new land. Some died shortly after their arrival. Life was a constant struggle to survive with precious little time for Anne to cultivate or contemplate beauty as her spirit longed to do.

Added to those burdens was the constant bickering among Massachusetts Bay Colony members. Every time she turned around, Anne heard new charges of heresy. She listened to the reports in fascination, wondering if her frequent doubts about God and the Puritan way showed.

At times the transplanted Englishwoman thought she would burst with frustration, doubt and fear. When that happened, she vented her feelings through writing poetry about her experiences. Those creative, life-giving sessions restored Anne to a certain quietness that kept her going in the barren wilderness the Puritans called the promised land. And while she dreamed of some day sharing her poetic scribblings with her children and other family members, Anne Bradstreet never imagined that she was on her way to becoming America's first published poet.

Thomas Dudley, chief steward and friend to the Puritan Earl of Lincoln, was careful to choose the right people for his staff. The nobleman had been good to Dudley, an orphan who had made something of his life. When Dudley's time came to find a protegé, he quickly chose Simon Bradstreet, an impressive young man with both bachelor's and master's degrees, who also had been orphaned in childhood. Thomas' wife, Dorothy Yorke Dudley, agreed. The more Dudley thought about it, the more he realized that Simon wasn't only an excellent prospect as a colleague, he was good husband material for Dudley's daughter, Anne.

In 1628 Anne, sixteen, and Simon Bradstreet, twenty-five, married in Northampton,

England. Times were difficult as the state's noose tightened around the Puritans, restricting their lives in a futile effort to shepherd them back into the Anglican fold. There were many family discussions about the wisdom of staying in England. Anne loved her homeland, but she understood the need for people to worship as their consciences dictated. Therefore, when her father and Simon decided they would emigrate to America, she acquiesced.

Their ship, *Arbella*, left England on March 20, 1630. They arrived three months later in a heavily wooded, mysterious land. After trying out a few different locations, the Bradstreets chose Merrimac (present-day Andover, Massachusetts) as their permanent home.

Anne's spirit troubled her for a long time after coming to America. She wasn't sure she would ever adjust to the primitive conditions or develop a steady faith. She couldn't openly express her doubts or fears either—not when her husband and father were prominent community figures, men who each went on to the governorship of Massachusetts Bay Colony. To express what she was going through, the young woman wrote poetry in which she described her "sinkings and droopings" of mind, body and spirit. Anne wrestled as well with the truth of Scripture, whether Bible miracles actually happened and if God really existed. Sometimes she even wondered whether the Roman Catholics and not the Puritans were Christ's true followers.

Yet Anne Bradstreet couldn't help believing. At the heart of it all, open rebellion not only didn't suit her station in life, it also didn't suit her spirit. She simply didn't have the disposition to reject God. Anne was like Peter who once asked Jesus, "Lord, to whom shall we go? You have the words of eternal life" (John 6:68).

Years later in a message to her children that looked back on that period of her life, Anne wrote:

> That there is a God my Reason would soon tell me by the wondrous workes that I see, the vast frame of the Heaven and the Earth, the order of all things, night and day, Summer and Winter, Spring and Autumne, the dayly providing for this great houshold upon the Earth, the preserving and directing of All to its proper end.[1]

Anne Bradstreet was a doubter who ultimately became reconciled to Christ.[2] Once she had resolved her spiritual doubts, Anne clung tenaciously to God throughout her life, in periods of illness and in the early deaths of children and grandchildren.

As she steadily gained spiritual ground, Anne wrote more mature poetry, and God's love resonated throughout it. "Like that of the pilgrim, the path of the poet led steadily upward: from rebellion to assurance, from immaturity to maturity."[3]

Like other Puritans, Anne was vitally interested in science, medicine, politics and social reform, which all helped make up God's fascinating world. These themes presented themselves in her poems. Above all, though, she wrote about the Christian life, family, everyday happenings, nature and committed love. The deep affection that she and Simon shared flows through Anne's poetry.

Her brother-in-law became fascinated with her work. The Reverend John Woodbridge decided that when he returned to England for a visit in 1647, he would take a manuscript of Anne's poems with him. (She had made some copies for close friends and family.) He regarded his sister-in-law as a pleasant aberration because Puritans believed that women's brains weren't designed to contemplate intellectual matters for long periods.

Due to Woodbridge's efforts, Anne Bradstreet's poems were published in England in 1650. Entitled *The Tenth Muse Lately Sprung Up in America*, the volume made Anne the first British American to publish a book of poetry. She was also the first Englishwoman to publish a significant volume of verse.

At first Anne was shocked by this turn of events. She had no idea that Woodbridge was going to do such a thing, and the notoriety embarrassed her deeply. Some of her fellow Puritans disapproved of her writing because they thought she neglected her eight children to do it.

But more than that, Anne knew those poems had been largely amateurish scribblings. She had meant them only for her children, close friends and relatives. She was far from being a Muse. Added to those factors was the profusion of typos and other misprintings in the book that made Anne cringe with embarrassment. She immediately set out to edit the volume. In 1678 a new edition of *The Tenth Muse* was published in America and included several of her later, more original and lyrical poems.

Although Anne came on the literary scene over a century before the Romantic poets or the Transcendentalists, she anticipated them. Her portrayal of the struggle between herself and her environment, as well as her emphasis on God's handiwork in nature, were themes that permeated the works of those later artists. It remains unclear, however, how much of an influence her poetry had on them.

The American scholar Samuel Eliot Morison believed that Anne Bradstreet was America's greatest female poet before Emily Dickinson. He also recognized the centrality of her faith in her life and writing:

> Physically weak she was, but morally robust. Imagine a gentlewoman in her position in the eighteenth or nineteenth century, living under pioneer conditions without the slightest hope of returning to the stately home of her youth, bearing eight

children with little or no medical aid, suffering frequent illness, fainting fits, and finally a wasting consumption. . . . Her art was not an escape from life, but an expression of life. It was shot through and through with her religious faith; a faith that made weak women strong, taught them to face life and take what came without flinching, as the inscrutable decree of a just God. . . . [S]he could employ every adversity to some spiritual advantage, and make good come out of evil. . . . Her life was proof, if it were needed, that creative art may be furthered by religion; and that even the duties of a housewife and mother in a new country cannot quench the sacred flame.[4]

In spite of Anne Bradstreet's prominence among American women, no portraits exist of her, and no one knows her exact burial place. She died in North Andover, Massachusetts on September 16, 1672 at the age of sixty.

Endnotes

1. Piercy, Josephine K. *Anne Bradstreet* (New York: Twayne Publishers, Inc. 1965), p. 98.
2. Ibid., p. 25.
3. Ibid., p. 41.
4. Morison, Samuel Eliot. *Builders of the Bay Colony* (Boston: Houghton Mifflin, 1930), pp. 333, 335-336.

FANNY CROSBY

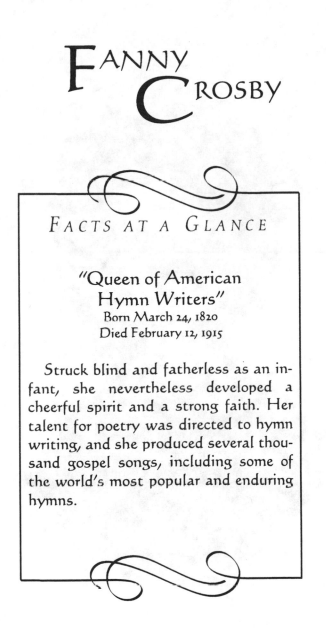

FACTS AT A GLANCE

"Queen of American Hymn Writers"
Born March 24, 1820
Died February 12, 1915

Struck blind and fatherless as an infant, she nevertheless developed a cheerful spirit and a strong faith. Her talent for poetry was directed to hymn writing, and she produced several thousand gospel songs, including some of the world's most popular and enduring hymns.

FANNY CROSBY

A Perth Amboy, New Jersey cabby, pulled his horse and buggy to the roadside after a clergyman signaled him. "Railroad station, if you please," he called out. The hackman watched with mild interest as the minister helped an aged blind woman into the cab. She was rather strange-looking in clothes of a different era as well as heavy green glasses. Although she was almost totally bent over, she spoke in clear, robust tones to the pastor when they got underway. The driver listened with not a small degree of interest to their conversation as the woman held her own in a spirited theological discussion. The coachman was amazed that in 1910 there could be such a woman. Noticing this, the minister smiled and said, "You may be wondering who this fine woman is."

"Well, uh, yes, sir, I was at that." The man felt like the boy whose mother found his hand in the cookie jar.

"This is Fanny Crosby, the hymn writer," explained the pastor. The hackman unexpectedly burst into tears. He couldn't drive like that, so he pulled the cab over to the side. "I'm sorry," he stuttered after a few minutes. "I'll get you to the station straightaway." In his mind, the driver knew there was someone who just had to meet Miss Crosby.

When they arrived at the railroad depot, the driver's eyes searched the throng until he found a certain young policeman. Pulling up to his uniformed friend, he called out, "This is Miss Fanny Crosby that wrote 'Safe in the Arms of Jesus.' I want you to help this pastor get her safely to the train."

The officer's mouth dropped. When he found his voice he told Fanny Crosby, "We sang that hymn last week—at my little girl's funeral."

The elderly song writer took his big hand in her frail ones. "My boy, God bless your dear heart! You shall have my prayers! And tell your wife that your sweet little girl is safe in the arms of Jesus."

The policeman could not contain his tears. He didn't even try.[1]

Frances Jane Crosby was born in Southeast,

New York, Putnam County in 1820, the only
child of John and Mercy Crosby. At the age of
six weeks, "Fanny" came down with an eye in-
flammation, and a physician prescribed hot
poultices that left the infant incurably blind,
only able to detect light and color. Less than a
year later, Fanny's father died.

Not even these early tragedies could blunt
the girl's cheerful spirit, however. As she grew,
she developed a love for riding horses and
climbing trees. Fanny often led her friends into
playful mischief. "Never self-pitying, she had
developed an acute ear and a phenomenal
memory to compensate for her blindness."[2] At
age eight she wrote a poem in which she expressed her view of life:

> Oh, what a happy soul am I!
> Although I cannot see,
> I am resolved that in this world
> Contented I will be.
>
> How many blessings I enjoy,
> That other people don't;
> To weep and sigh because I'm blind,
> I cannot, and I won't![3]

According to one biographer, "By her brave
and sunny disposition and trust in Jesus, this
little blind girl, who would not 'weep and sigh
because I'm blind,' has inspired millions of
people to useful, happy lives."[4]

Fanny Crosby was educated largely by her mother and grandmother during her childhood. The latter took a special interest in teaching Fanny about the world of nature, and the girl developed a special love for astronomy and horticulture. Fanny's grandmother also made sure that the child knew the Bible thoroughly. Fanny could repeat from memory huge portions of it, including many Psalms, Proverbs, the books of Ruth and the Song of Solomon and the first five books of the Old Testament.[5] Fanny remained utterly devoted to the Scriptures throughout adulthood. She once said, "All that I am, and all that I expect to be, in literature or in life, is due to the Bible."[6]

Fanny Crosby moved with her family to Ridgefield, Connecticut when she was nine. At fifteen she entered the New York Institution for the Blind where she hoped to fulfill an ardent desire to learn more about the arts and sciences. Fanny's teachers quickly discouraged her from writing poetry, however. Then a Scottish phrenologist—one who studies the skull's formation as an indication of intellect and character—visited the school. After examining Fanny's head, George Combe declared that she had a gift for poetry. The school's administration took this to heart and from then on encouraged Fanny's poetic talent, often showcasing her in school exhibitions. She often recited for visiting dignitaries and performed while traveling to Hudson River towns by canalboat to promote the school's mission. She even addressed both Houses of Congress, once in January 1844, then in April 1847, and met President Polk at the White House.

Miss Crosby began writing for newspapers and magazines around 1841 when a eulogy for President Harrison appeared in the *New York Herald.* She also published articles and poetry with the *Saturday Evening Post,* the *Clinton Signal* and the *Fireman's Journal.* One commentator noted, "Her verses were seriously flawed by the sentimental affectations of the day, but her prosody evinces more than amateur skill."[7]

From 1847 until 1858 Crosby taught English grammar and rhetoric, as well as ancient history, at her alma mater. She also wrote four collections of poetry between 1844 and 1858 besides many popular songs, including "There's Music in the Air" and "Hazel Dell." Crosby earned almost $3,000 in royalties for her "Rosalie, the Prairie Flower." She and composer George F. Root collaborated on a cantata, "The Flower Queen," in 1851. She became quite a celebrity.

Curiously the future President Grover Cleveland, whose brother was the New York Institution for the Blind's head teacher, served as the assistant to the superintendent during Crosby's tenure there. One of his duties was to take her dictation.

At thirty-eight Fanny Crosby married a former student, Alexander Van Alstyne, who had become a music teacher and church organist.

They lived in Brooklyn, and her husband composed some music for a few of her hymns, insisting that she continue writing under "Crosby." Little is known about him based on his wife's autobiographies, but they had a child who died as an infant. Van Alstyne passed away in 1902.

In 1864 Fanny wrote the first of thousands of hymns after composer W.D. Bradbury suggested that she try some gospel songs. She was delighted to oblige. During her life she wrote between 5,500 and 9,000 hymns, words that frequently came to her with stunning quickness. She said that on some days she wrote up to seven of them, while on others, nothing came to her. "Safe in the Arms of Jesus" took Crosby only fifteen minutes. One biographer said, "No such phenomenon had occurred since the days of Isaac Watts and Charles Wesley."[8] It is difficult to determine exactly how many hymns Fanny Crosby wrote because she used upward of 200 pseudonyms to protect her modesty. She confessed to sometimes taking too much pride in her considerable achievements. In her life she collaborated with over twenty composers, including evangelist Dwight L. Moody's renowned associate, Ira D. Sankey.

Fanny Crosby often referred to blindness in her hymns. For example, in "All the Way My Saviour Leads Me" she describes the importance of a guiding hand to one who is blind, especially in the line, "Though my weary steps may falter."[9] In "Pass Me Not, O Gentle Saviour" there is a veiled reference to the biblical story of Blind Bartimaeus' encounter with Jesus.

Millions of people around the world sang Fanny's songs of a joyous and abiding faith, with many of her compositions translated into other languages. Whenever a new female talent emerged in gospel songwriting, she was inevitably called "the British Fanny Crosby" or "the Swedish Fanny Crosby." Her music reached the remotest parts of the world as well. One story told of travelers who heard Arab bedouins sing Crosby's "Saved by Grace."[10] And at President Grant's funeral, the bands continually played "Safe in the Arms of Jesus."

Of course, Crosby had her critics. S.A.W. Duffield remarked, "It is more to Mrs. Van Alstyne's credit that she had occasionally found a pearl than that she had brought to the surface so many oyster shells."[11] "Julian" wrote that Fanny Crosby's hymns were "with few exceptions very weak and poor, their simplicity and earnestness being their redeeming features. Their popularity is largely due to the melodies to which they are wedded."[12] According to Clifford E. Rinehart, "Critics of hymnody generally agree that few of her hymns possess any literary value; like her verses, they rely too heavily upon the cliché."[13] Another reviewer was kinder: "Like her poetry, her hymns suffered generally from cliché and sentimentality, but they also displayed an occasional gleam of more than ordinary talent."[14]

Regardless, Fanny Crosby touched—and continues to touch in countless hymnbooks of the Christian faith—millions of people with her simple compositions. The late nineteenth century social worker Ann Cobham wrote, "(Her) hymns have brought solace and enheartment to millions. They are songs that will never die."[15] Evangelist and hymn writer George Coles Stebbins said, "There was probably no writer in her day who appealed more to the valid experience of the Christian life or who expressed more sympathetically the deep longings of the human heart than Fanny Crosby."[16] William Jensen, the Baptist hymnologist, commented that Fanny Crosby "to a greater extent than any other person . . . captured the spirit of literary expression of the Gospel-song era."[17]

"She was one of the three most prominent figures (D.L. Moody and Ira Sankey were the others) in American evangelical religious life in the last quarter of the nineteenth century."[18] Indeed, Sankey and Moody attributed much of their success at evangelistic meetings to her hymns and how God used them to touch people's hearts.

Although Crosby wrote for all Christians, the Methodist Church especially cherished her as

one of its own. She had been raised in the
Presbyterian Church, but left it in 1850. For
years the Methodists observed an annual
Fanny Crosby Day.

Crosby spent a happy and healthy old age
with a widowed sister in Bridgeport, Connecticut. She wrote two books about her life and
often spoke at New York's Bowery Mission and
at the Y.M.C.A.'s railroad branches. At ninety-
four she suffered from a fatal cerebral hemor-
rhage and arteriosclerosis. Fanny Crosby is
buried at Mount Grove Cemetery in Bridgeport.

Books by Fanny Crosby:

The Blind Girl and Other Poems (1844)
Monterey and Other Poems (1851)
A Wreath of Columbia's Flowers (1858)
Bells at Evening and Other Verses (1897)
Fanny Crosby's Life Story by Herself (1903)
Memories of Eighty Years (1906)

Endnotes

1. Ruffin, Bernard. *Fanny Crosby* (Philadelphia:
   United Church Press, 1976), p. 13.
2. Rinehart, Clifford E. article in James, James, and
   Boyer, Eds. *Notable American Women* (Cambridge:
   Belknap Press, 1971), p. 412.
3. Rudin, Cecelia Margaret. *Stories of Hymns We Love*
   (Chicago: John Rudin & Company Inc., 1951), p.
   76.

   4. Ibid., p. 68.
   5. Rothwell, Helen F. *Fanny Crosby: A Great Poetess*
      (Wheaton, IL: Van Kampen Press, 1944), p. 5.
   6. Ibid., p. 5.
   7. Rinehart, p. 411.
   8. Johnson, Allen and Malone, Dumas. *Dictionary of
      American Biography* (New York: Charles Scribner's
      Sons, 1958), p. 567.
   9. The Hymnbook, p. 365.
  10. Ruffin, p. 15.
  11. Johnson, p. 567.
  12. Ibid., p. 567.
  13. Rinehart, p. 412.
  14. McHenry, Robert, ed. *Famous American Women*
      (New York: Dover, 1980), p. 87.
  15. Ruffin, p. 14.
  16. Ibid., p. 15.
  17. Ibid., p. 15.
  18. Ibid., p. 15.

JULIA WARD HOWE

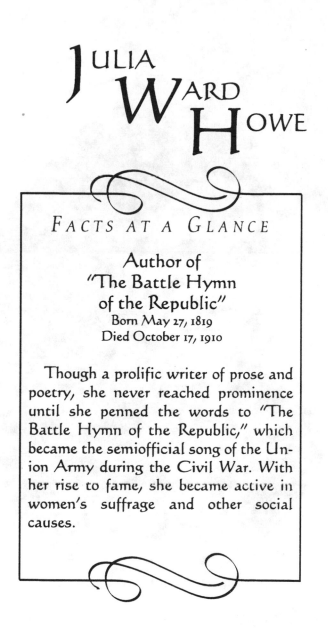

FACTS AT A GLANCE

Author of
"The Battle Hymn
of the Republic"
Born May 27, 1819
Died October 17, 1910

Though a prolific writer of prose and poetry, she never reached prominence until she penned the words to "The Battle Hymn of the Republic," which became the semiofficial song of the Union Army during the Civil War. With her rise to fame, she became active in women's suffrage and other social causes.

JULIA WARD HOWE

The Civil War had broken out, and Julia Ward Howe threw herself into the Union cause. She organized many of Boston's churchwomen into groups, one for sewing, one for rolling bandages, another for making jams and jellies for the troops. She also wrote plays for her daughters to perform at Union fund-raisers.

When her husband, the illustrious Dr. Samuel Gridley Howe, asked Julia to accompany him to Washington to meet the President, she heartily agreed. Seeing Abraham Lincoln was not, however, the highlight of her trip.

While Julia and her husband went off to a place near the Potomac River to review the troops, a minor skirmish broke out between those Union soldiers and some Confederates who were in the vicinity, interrupting the parade. The onlookers grew excited and somewhat frightened until the "all-clear" came. The Union outfit was safe, and so were their reviewers. The scuffle had created a major traffic jam, however, and to pass the time, Julia sang to the servicemen. They loved her rendition of the popular "John Brown's Body Lies A-Mouldering in the Grave."

"Julia," a friend of hers said, "that tune is so pretty, but the words are so base. Why don't you write better ones to it?"

The poet became thoughtful. "I'll see what I can do," she smiled.

That night in her Washington hotel room, Julia awakened with those new words in her heart. She didn't want to disturb Samuel, and, as she often did at home while getting an inspiration during the night, Julia groped for a pencil and piece of paper on her bed stand. In the darkness she scribbled the words that came to her, line after line.

When she got up the next morning, Julia felt as if the experience had been a dream. Yet on her night table were the words to the "John Brown's Body" tune. Back in Boston she carefully wrote them out and sent them to *Atlantic Monthly* magazine. The editors decided to use it, calling the piece "The Battle Hymn of the Republic" and publishing it on the front page of the February 1862 issue. They paid her $10 for it. The poem became a national sensation. President Lincoln loved it so much that when

he first heard it sung, he is said to have wept
while requesting, "Sing that prayer again."[1]

Mine eyes have seen the glory
   of the coming of the Lord;
He is trampling out the vintage
   where the grapes of wrath are stored;
He hath loosed the fateful lightning
   of His terrible swift sword;
His truth is marching on,

I have seen Him in the watch fires
   of a hundred circling camps;
They have builded Him an altar
   in the evening dews and damps;
I can read His righteous sentence
   by the dim and flaring lamps.
His day is marching on.

I have read a fiery gospel,
   writ in burnished rows of steel:
"As ye deal with my contemners,
   so with you my grace shall deal;
Let the Hero, born of woman,
   crush the serpent with his heel
Since God is marching on."

He has sounded forth the trumpet
   that shall never call retreat;
He is sifting out the hearts of men
   before His judgment seat:
Oh, be swift, my soul, to answer Him!

Be jubilant, my feet!
Our God is marching on.

In the beauty of the lilies,
   Christ was born across the sea,
With a glory in His bosom
   that transfigures you and me:
As He died to make men holy,
   let us die to make men free,
While God is marching on.[2]

———⟨✦⟩———

Julia Rush Cutler and Samuel Ward, Jr.
lived amongst New York's social elite in the
early nineteenth century. Samuel was a partner in a Wall Street banking firm and a
staunch Episcopalian who insisted on family
prayers at breakfast. His bright and spunky
daughter, Julia, often chafed at her nurse's di-
rectives to be a proper little girl. Instead she
enjoyed playing loudly with her brothers. She
also showed such intellectual promise and determination that Julia's father engaged private
tutors to instruct her in Latin, French, German, art and dancing. This went far beyond
the usual sewing and piano lessons given to
other wealthy young women.
   In spite of her mother's death from tuberculosis when Julia was five, the child's early years
were stable and happy, largely due to the presence of boisterous aunts and uncles. There

were lively parties and exciting vacations as well.

Julia Ward loved literature and began writing her own poems and essays for magazines at sixteen. She never put her name to her work, however, since editors did not encourage females in their literary pursuits. Readers would no doubt have been astonished to find that the author of essays on Goethe, Schiller and Lamartine in the *New York Review* and *Theological Review* had been written by a young woman.[3]

In 1843 Ward family friend Henry Wadsworth Longfellow introduced Julia to Dr. Samuel Gridley Howe, then forty years old and head of the Perkins Institute for the Blind in Boston. Howe had gained fame through teaching the blind, deaf and mute Laura Bridgman to speak, as well as through his heroic escapades in the Greek Revolution. Julia and Howe were married on April 23, 1843. They enjoyed a lengthy European honeymoon before residing in Boston at a home they called "Green Peace" for its profusion of trees. All was not peaceful for Julia in Boston, however. At that time Bostonians and New Yorkers did not mix well. In addition, other women roundly criticized the absent-minded woman for her poor housekeeping and unconventional child-rearing methods. Julia refused to employ nurses or governesses, and she insisted on writing for two hours every day while her children entertained themselves.

In 1854 Mrs. Howe's first volume of poetry, *Passion Flowers*, appeared. She also published *Words for the Hour, Leonora, or The World's Own* (a play that ran in New York), and *A Trip to Cuba*. None of these became major successes. For a while she and Dr. Howe also produced an abolitionist newspaper called *The Commonwealth*, but he did not like involving Julia in public affairs and kept her on the fringes of the enterprise. Their marriage soured, but they stayed together. On their twentieth anniversary Julia wrote in her journal:

> In the course of that time I have never known my husband to approve of any act of mine which I myself valued. . . . [E]v-erything has been contemptible in his eyes because [it was] not his way of doing things. . . .[4]

Only later in their lives would that change.

In 1861 Dr. and Mrs. Howe traveled to Washington, D.C. where they met President Lincoln at the outset of the Civil War. During the trip, Julia was inspired to write "The Battle Hymn of the Republic." It became a semiofficial song of the Union Army, and it made her so famous that it took her breath away. Just after the war when she appeared at a social function in New York City, the master of ceremonies amazed Julia by introducing her as the woman who had written "the greatest song of the war."[5] With her rising celebrity, Mrs.

Howe became active in the fight for women's suffrage. In 1868 the New England Women Suffrage Association chose her as its president. She also supported the New England and General Federation of Women's Clubs, as well as the Association of Advancement of Women, which promoted pioneering women in the ministry, law, education and science. Julia herself frequently preached in churches, although she was never ordained. She once said of this, "It was borne in upon me that I had much to say to my day and generation which could not and should not be communicated in rhyme."[6] Julia's main concern as a woman was "to keep up the tone of society."[7]

In 1870 she wrote "Appeal to Womanhood Throughout the World" and became the president of the Women's International Peace Association's American division the following year. In spite of her pacifism, however, Julia Ward Howe supported an American military warning against the Turks during a 1903 crisis, to the point of calling for an actual battle. She wrote, "Our own warship is where it should be. I would to God that we might hear the thunder of its guns."[8] She said that her greatest hope for peace lay in the unification of Protestant Christians throughout the world so they could redeem oppressed peoples from despotism. "This cannot be done without armed authority," she admitted, "but it can be done without bloodshed." She did not explain how that could be accomplished.[9]

In addition to her social activism, Mrs. Howe continued to write poetry, travel books and essays. She also founded a literary journal, *Northern Lights*, which lasted for just eleven issues, as well as *The Woman's Journal,* a suffrage-oriented newspaper. She served as its editor for twenty years.

Julia and her husband experienced a full reconciliation as they grew older and he gradually supported her public activities. He died in January 1876. She wrote of him, "All that is most sterling in American character may be said to have found its embodiment in Dr. Howe."[10]

In 1908 the American Academy of Arts and Letters elected Julia Ward Howe to its all-male circle. That same year she had an extraordinary experience that reinforced the belief of many people that the twentieth century truly would be "the Christian century," as many religious leaders had prophesied. Julia had awakened during the night with a penetrating and illuminating idea. She called it "An account of my vision of the world regenerated by the combined labor and love of Men and Women":

> Men and women of every clime [were] working like bees to unwrap the evils of society and to discover the whole web of vice and misery and to apply the remedies and also to find the influences that should best counteract the evil and its attendant suffering. . . . All were advancing with one

end in view, one foe to trample, one ever-lasting goal to gain. . . . And then I saw the victory. All of evil was gone from the earth. Misery was blotted out. Mankind was emancipated and ready to march forward in a new Era of human understanding, all-encompassing sympathy and ever-present help, the Era of perfect love, of peace passing understanding. [11]

The highly esteemed writer and reformer traveled widely until the infirmities of age overtook her, then remained active in public life through her publications. Julia Ward Howe died of pneumonia on October 17, 1910 at her cottage in Newport, Rhode Island four years before World War I.

Other books by Julia Ward Howe:

From the Oak to the Olive (1868)
Modern Society (1880)
Margaret Fuller (1883)
Is Polite Society Polite? (1895)
From Sunset Ridge: Poems Old and New (1898)
Reminiscences (1899)
At Sunset (1910)

Endnotes

1. Wagoner, Jean Brown. *Julia Ward Howe: Girl of Old New York* (Cornwall, NY: The Cornwall Press, 1945), p. 203.
2. Ibid., pp. 205-206.

3. Boyer, Paul S. Article in *Notable American Women*, ed. James, James and Boyer (Cambridge: Belknap Press, 1971), p. 226.
4. Ibid.
5. Wagoner, p. 204.
6. Clifford, Deborah Pickman. *Mine Eyes Have Seen the Glory: A Biography of Julia Ward Howe* (Boston: Little, Brown and Company, 1978), p. 159.
7. Boyer, p. 228.
8. Ibid.
9. Clifford, p. 268.
10. Boyer, p. 228.
11. Clifford, p. 270.

KAAHUMANU

FACTS AT A GLANCE

Hawaiian Queen,
Champion of Christianity
Born 1768(?)
Died June 5, 1832

A powerful and influential ruler of Hawaii during a time of great social upheaval, she helped unify the islands and elevate the position of women in Hawaiian society. Following her conversion to Christianity, she was a faithful witness to her people and a helper of Prostestant missionaries.

(The illustration is an artist's rendition; no portraits are available.

KAAHUMANU

———

During King Kamehameha's rule of Hawaii, he relied heavily on the advice of his dynamic and much younger wife, Kaahumanu. When he died in 1819, his widow became *kuhina nui*, or co-ruler, with Kamehameha's son by another marriage. A curious situation followed, however, when the new king traveled to England in 1823 and died there a year later. Kaahumanu now took center stage in controlling the islands as Queen Regent on behalf of the very young Kamehameha III. That was the unmistakable message she sent during her glorious inauguration:

The ceremony of installation was a gorgeous spectacle. Along the shore, partly on the sand and partly in the water, was a great throng of people; facing them, a group of chiefs, resplendent in feather cloaks and helmets, with the dowager

Queen Kaahumanu occupying the central position.[1]

Kaahumanu left no doubt as to who was in charge of the Hawaiian Islands.

Kaahumanu's birth date is not known for certain, but scholars place it between 1768 and 1777. Many legends surround her infancy. For instance, some say that she was born in a cave at Hana on Maui during a war between rival chiefs.[2] Other tales recount several close calls Kaahumanu had with death, including one in which she was swept out to sea. What is known for sure is that Kaahumanu's mother had once been married to a king of Maui, long before Hawaiian unification, and that her father, Keeaumoku, served as an advisor to King Kamehameha.

Kaahumanu grew into a formidable woman. A person of great inner strength, she also stood six feet tall and weighed 300 pounds—and in her culture, was considered very attractive. The explorer Captain George Vancouver considered Kaahumanu "one of the finest women we had yet seen on any of the islands."[3] As a passionate young teenager she married King Kamehameha, to whom she had been promised as a child by her father. Her husband, a middle-aged man with many other wives, professed that he loved Kaahumanu best.

Theirs was not only a meeting of two great minds and hearts, but a locking of horns as well. Their mutual stubbornness resulted at least once in their estrangement, with Kaahumanu returning to her parents' home. Captain Vancouver, who was fond of both, helped reconcile them.

Following her husband's death, Kaahumanu married the king of Kauai, Kaumualii, on October 9, 1821. Within a short time she also wed his son, Kealiiahonui. In 1822 she and Kaumualii spent several months touring the islands with an entourage numbering roughly 1,000. Such journeys helped cement their subjects' loyalty, but they also frequently resulted in severe food shortages for the locals. (After Christian missionaries encouraged her to be monogamous, Kaahumanu abandoned her marriage to her stepson.) She had no children by any of her marriages.

This powerful woman lived during a time of upheaval and transition in her nation's history. Outside pressures threatened the political autonomy of Hawaii; on the other hand, there was a strong internal movement toward unifying the various islands into a single kingdom. Kaahumanu was also anxious to elevate the position of women in Hawaiian society; until that time, they were not even permitted to eat with men. Kaahumanu convinced Kamehameha II to break that ban, declaring that she was going to do it regardless. The turning point came in November 1819:

> When the young king had finally made his decision and was on the point of putting it into execution—a course requiring no small amount of courage on his part—he caused a feast to be prepared at Kailua, to which all the leading chiefs and several foreigners were invited. Two tables were set in the European fashion, one for men and one for women.
>
> After the guests were seated, and had begun to eat, the king took two or three turns round each table, as if to see what passed at each; and then suddenly, and without any previous warning to any but those in secret, seated himself in a vacant chair at the women's table, and began to eat voraciously, but was evidently much perturbed. The guests, astonished at this act, clapped their hands, and cried out, "Ai noa—the eating tabu is broken."[4]

Following this deed, popular revolts against the traditional religion with its discriminatory bans broke out. When Protestant missionaries arrived a year later from New England, Hawaiians were largely open to Christianity, which elevated the status of women. (The country became officially "Christian" in 1840.)

Kaahumanu had become literate under missionary guidance, but wrestled with accepting Christianity for four years. During that period, however, she instituted a law code based largely on the Ten Commandments. The strong-willed ruler considered it time for her subjects to abandon archaic and detrimental principles. She believed that Christianity provided the foundation for a better, more equitable society. In June 1824 Kaahumanu announced the creation of her law code that proscribed:

There shall be no murder.
There shall be no theft of any description.
There shall be no boxing or fighting among the people.
There shall be no work or play on the Sabbath, but this day shall be regarded as the sacred day of Jehovah.[5]

When Lord Byron visited Hawaii as a British emissary the following year, he learned of this code and lent his enthusiastic support. This was of great value to Kaahumanu because the king would have to lend final approval, and the chiefs of her people would have to support the laws to make them viable. There was considerable debate among the chiefs of her people about basing her laws on the Ten Commandments, and Kamehameha III had doubts. Byron suggested that the new laws include a provision for trial by jury in capital cases, but no formal action was taken until 1830.[6]

At the end of 1827 the king decided to establish three laws for the time being: prohibitions against murder, stealing and adultery. His final word came down on October 7, 1829, reflecting Kaahumanu's considerable influence on him: "The laws of my country prohibit murder, theft, adultery, fornication, retailing ardent spirits at houses for selling spirits, amusements on the Sabbath day, gambling and betting on the Sabbath day and at all times."[7]

Kaahumanu, one of Hawaii's most powerful rulers, had set the stage for the Christianization of her people.

Meanwhile, she had submitted to baptism in 1825, taking Elizabeth as her Christian name. Her subjects referred to her as "the new Kaahumanu" because of her evangelical fervor for converting her people. She ordered the demolition of pagan idols and would not permit Roman Catholic missionaries to come into Hawaii, fearing that their statues would pull her people back into idol worship. Kaahumanu also supported temperance, to the extent of ordering the destruction of sugarcane fields so that no more rum could be produced.

In her final years, Kaahumanu traveled widely throughout the islands meeting her subjects and promoting Christianity and literacy. She died on June 5, 1832 in Manoa Valley, Honolulu, having been buried next to Kamehameha I, the most imposing figure among the native rulers of Hawaii.

A chief of high rank and autocratic temper, she governed her people, as a contemporary observer remarked, "with a rod of iron," but in her later years her most striking characteristic was religious zeal. She was the firm friend and protector of the Protestant missionaries and exerted herself to the time of her last illness in spreading the Christian gospel. Henry A. Pierce, a frequent critic of the Protestant missionaries and the native rulers, wrote of Kaahumanu just after her death:

She died a *Christian*. It has always heretofore been my opinion that her adherence and adoption of the Christian religion was from policy . . . but I have lately been convinced from the piety displayed during her sickness and at the hour of her death that she really believed in and practiced the principles of the Christian religion.[8]

Endnotes

1. Kuykendall, Ralph S. *The Hawaiian Kingdom: Volume 1, 1778-1854, Foundation and Transformation* (Honolulu: University of Hawaii Press, 1938), p. 63.
2. Allen, Gwenfread, article in James, James and Boyer, eds. *Notable American Women* (Cambridge: Belknap Press, 1971), p. 301.

3. Kuykendall, p. 40.
4. Ibid., p. 68.
5. Ibid., p. 118.
6. Ibid., p. 120.
7. Ibid., p. 126.
8. Ibid., p. 133.

HELEN KELLER

FACTS AT A GLANCE

**Author, Lecturer,
Advocate for the Disabled**
Born June 27, 1880
Died June 1, 1968

In an era when multiple-handicapped people were considered unteachable, she became a college graduate and a popular writer and speaker. Her autobiography in particular, with its insight into the world of the severly disabled, gained her worldwide fame.

HELEN KELLER

The first meeting of Helen Keller and her teacher, Annie Sullivan, did not go well. The six-year-old, who was blind, deaf and mute, threw a rousing tantrum. Annie quickly assessed the situation. The Kellers had let Helen do whatever she pleased to try to make up for the little girl's cataclysmic losses. Miss Sullivan suggested that they let her and Helen move into a small cottage near the house where she would have full authority over Helen. They reluctantly agreed.

Annie spent several days getting Helen under control while spelling into the child's hand everything they did and experienced. Although Helen proved a quick study, she learned everything by rote. And then, on a day of miserable frustration, something wonderful happened. A breakthrough! As Annie and Helen went for a walk, the teacher saw someone working a hand

pump. She took Helen over to it and put the
child's hands under the sparkling cascade.
Years later Helen Keller remembered the impact of that experience and wrote:

> [A]s the cool stream gushed over one
> hand, she spelled into the other the word
> water, first slowly, then rapidly. I stood
> still, my whole attention fixed upon the
> motions of her fingers. I knew then that
> W-A-T-E-R meant the wonderful cool
> something that was flowing over my
> hand. As we returned to the house every
> object I touched seemed to quiver with
> life.[1]

Helen had passed from darkness to light.

Helen Adams Keller was born in Tuscumbia,
Alabama to Kate Adams Keller, who came
from a well-to-do family, and Captain Arthur
H. Keller. He was a Civil War veteran who became a newspaper editor, then a U.S. Marshall. At the age of nineteen months Helen
suffered an illness, possibly scarlet fever, that
left her blind, deaf and mute. The little girl became unmanageable, clawing and kicking at
people, engaging in appalling displays of temper. Still, she could communicate by using
more than sixty signals for people and things.

She pretended, for example, to put on glasses when referring to her father, and swept up her hair for her mother. Shivering meant she wanted ice cream.

When Helen was six, her father contacted the inventor Alexander Graham Bell. Bell's son-in-law, Michael Anagnos, ran the Perkins Institution for the Blind in Boston, and Captain Keller hoped Bell could recommend a teacher for Helen. Anagnos became deeply interested in Helen's case. He sent Annie Sullivan, a twenty-year-old teacher at Perkins, to Alabama. Helen called the day Miss Sullivan arrived—March 3, 1887—her "soul's birthday." Annie spent the rest of her life, nearly fifty years, with Helen.

"Teacher," as Helen referred to her, showed the girl how to feel objects and connect them with words that Annie spelled on Helen's palm. The six-year-old also learned to read sentences by touching raised words on cardboard. In addition, Helen started making sentences with a grooved writing board. She put paper over it, then used her forefinger to guide a pencil point along the grooves so the letters came out neatly next to each other.

For the next few years Helen spent her winters at Perkins learning the system of Braille. Afterward Sarah Fuller of the Horace Mann School for the Deaf, also in Boston, began teaching Helen how to talk by "feeling the position of the tongue and lips, making sounds, and imitating the lip and tongue motions."[2] In addition Helen began lip reading by putting her fingers on the speaker's lips and throat while the words were spelled out for her.

She continued her education at the Wright-Humason School for the Deaf in New York when she was fourteen, then at the Cambridge School for Young Ladies in Massachusetts two years later. Annie Sullivan was her constant companion and they often had opportunities to meet famous people who had become interested in Helen's miraculous transformation. Included among them was Mark Twain, who once wrote Helen:

> You are a wonderful creature, the most wonderful in the world. You and your other half together—Miss Sullivan, I mean, for it took the pair of you to make a complete and perfect whole.[3]

Although Helen's religious training was unconventional (her father was a Presbyterian, her mother Episcopalian, but they had not taken her to church at all), she took to faith in God like a picture to a frame. When Helen and Annie were first paired, Michael Anagnos had instructed Miss Sullivan to let "Helen's religious ideas . . . develop from within instead of her taking them from without."[4] He felt that she had a natural bent toward religion and wanted to find out whether Helen was innately religious. He asked, "What shape might [her beliefs] take when freed of the supernaturalism of established creeds?"[5] Annie agreed to this.

When Helen was nine, however, one of her aunts tried to teach her the catechism. The child became very curious about God and, since Anagnos was away, Annie Sullivan decided to take Helen to Boston's Trinity Church. Pastor Phillips Brooks, who authored the hymn "O Little Town of Bethlehem," eagerly took Helen under his wing. Anagnos was not pleased, but Miss Sullivan declared that she was just as responsible for Helen's religious upbringing as he was and that Bishop Brooks was good for Helen. He had a powerful impact on the girl, so much so that she persuaded her parents to name their new baby after him. As an adult Helen remembered how he had sat her on his knees and told her very simply "the wonderful story of Jesus Christ, and my eyes filled with tears, and my heart beat with love for the gentle Nazarene who restored sight to the blind and speech to the mute, healed the sick, fed the hungry and turned sorrow into joy."[6] Brooks helped her understand "the central truth that God is Love and that His Love is the 'Light of all men.' "[7]

A few years later, however, one of Alexander Graham Bell's employees introduced Helen to the writings of religious philosopher Emmanuel Swedenborg, and she took a few steps away from Christian orthodoxy. Helen embraced

universalism, believing that anyone who believed in God and lived well would go to
heaven, as opposed to those who came to God
through Christ alone. Regardless, Helen did
not stray far from the teachings of her dear
shepherd Phillips Brooks. What primarily had
drawn her to Swedenborg was his fundamental
belief in the world "as a conflict between light
and darkness, God and the Devil," which was
something to which she strongly related.[8] In
addition, the Swede's emphasis on life after
death so reassured Helen that she did not fear
her own demise. "Life here," she once said, "is
more cruel than death—life divides and es-
tranges, while death, which at heart is life eternal, reunites and reconciles."[9]

In spite of Helen's physical limitations and
sufferings, her faith enabled her to view her future and the world's in a positive way. At fourteen she confided to her diary:

> This century—the wonderful nineteenth
> century—is nearing its end, and right in
> front of us stands the closed gate of the
> new century, on which in letters of light,
> God has written these words, "Here is the
> way to wisdom, virtue and happiness."
> What do you think this means, diary?
> Shall I tell you what I think it means?
> Why, these words, written on the gate of
> the new century, are a prophecy. They
> foretell that in the beautiful sometime all

wrong will be made right, and all the sorrows of life will find their fulfillment in perfect happiness. Do you not see now, diary, that the noblest dreams of the greatest and wisest of men are to be the realities of the future? So, we must trust God securely. We must not doubt Him because of the great mystery of pain, and sin, and death. Hope is our privilege and our duty. . . .

Hope makes me glad and content with my life, for I know that in God's beautiful sometime I shall have the things for which I pray now so earnestly—fullness; greatness and goodness of soul higher than all things. Yes! I know that they will all come sometimes, perhaps in this beautiful new century.[10]

She was at peace with her condition: "I thank God for my handicaps, for, through them, I have found myself, my work, and my God."[11]

In spite of Helen Keller's physical disadvantages, as a teenager she still struggled with the same growing-up issues as others her age—the search for independence and personal identity, the conflict between choosing the best in life over the expedient or base and arguments with her guardian. She noted:

Tonight I'm having a hard fight with—I don't know what—myself or some bad

fairy that doesn't love me. . . . I've been
so accustomed to neglect my studies! I've
left so many things poorly done—or not
done at all! Something in me resists
fiercely, and I can't explain it. But I'm
getting a clearer idea of the importance
of character. . . . Still, it is mighty hard to
keep from wandering away. . . .

Am I a bad girl after all? Or is it that
bad fairy that seems to want to spoil all I
do? Was it born in me, or did it slip in
when God wasn't looking? I wonder why
He doesn't kill it now? He is all love and
wisdom, "too pure to behold iniquity."
Why doesn't He pull me out of this bad
fairy's power when I WANT to get
away?[12]

Whatever restlessness and struggles challenged the teenage Helen Keller, however, she
developed into a brilliant scholar and entered
Radcliffe College. Annie Sullivan went with
her, dutifully spelling lectures and textbooks
into the student's hands. Besides her demanding studies, Helen also wrote a story about herself in 1891 for the *Ladies Home Journal*.
Publisher John Macy broke a taboo by printing
this article because it was about blindness; at
that time, the affliction was closely associated
with venereal disease. However, the piece was
so well-received that Helen wrote an autobiography, *The Story of My Life*, with Macy's assis-

tance. It was published while she was still a student at Radcliffe, making her wealthy and famous, her reputation stretching across the globe. "Keller was internationally perceived as an extraordinary example of the ability of humans to triumph over difficulties."[13] She graduated from Radcliffe with honors in 1904. The following year Annie married John Macy, and Helen went to live with them.

With school behind her, Helen wrote and lectured for a living, becoming a regular contributor to *The Century*, *McClure's* and *The Atlantic Monthly*, as well as the author of a dozen more books besides her autobiography. She traveled widely for the American Foundation for the Blind and campaigned for various social causes, some of which conflicted with popular opinion, such as birth control, women's suffrage and the abolishment of capital punishment. In addition, she became a socialist and spoke out against U.S. involvement in World War I. In spite of these departures from the majority opinion, however, she retained her popularity, largely because of her amazing courage in spite of tremendous odds.

Annie and John Macy eventually separated, and a Scotswoman named Polly Thomson began arranging Helen's travels, as well as her hair and her home. Another secretary, Peter Fagan, was employed when Helen and Annie became much in demand as speakers, but he didn't last. When Mrs. Keller learned that her daughter planned to elope with Fagan and drop Annie Sullivan altogether, she drove the young man away at gunpoint.

In 1918 a new motion picture, "Deliverance," portrayed Helen's struggle to overcome her handicaps. The film was not a success. To earn more money, Helen and Annie Sullivan developed a vaudeville routine, acting out the incredible story of their meeting and how Annie helped Helen escape her darkness.

In 1924 Keller became the American Foundation for the Blind's major advisor. She lobbied Congress for laws favorable to the blind, including the successful Pratt Bill, which established and funded reading services for the visually challenged. Her efforts also helped end the widespread and often senseless institutionalization of the handicapped, and she established commissions for the blind in thirty states as well. President Franklin D. Roosevelt, himself handicapped by polio, greatly admired her. He once said, "Anything Helen Keller is for, I am for."[14]

Annie Sullivan's sight had never been particularly strong, and in the 1930's she actually lost one eye. Since she could no longer help Helen with reading, Polly Thomson took on that responsibility. Annie did travel with them, however, including a trip to Europe where they met the King and Queen of England as well as other European royalty. Following unsuccessful surgery on her remaining eye, Sullivan weakened considerably and died in 1936. Helen's heart was broken, but not her dauntless spirit.

When World War II broke out in 1939, Helen abandoned her earlier pacifism. Seeing the evils of Adolf Hitler and the tragedy of Pearl Harbor, she said that only war could stop the carnage. That and faith which, she believed, "is the strength by which a shattered world shall emerge into the light."[15] She eagerly visited many soldiers who had been blinded in combat, providing tremendous encouragement for them. She told the public, "They do not want to be treated as heroes. They want to be able to live naturally and to be treated as human beings."[16] These visits were, she said, "the crowning experience of my life."[17]

Following the war, Helen Keller traveled throughout the world, visiting South Africa, the Middle East, Latin America, India and Japan. "The Unconquered," a movie about her life, was released in 1953 and won an Academy Award. Two years later she became the first woman to receive an honorary degree from Harvard. An even more successful play-turned-movie about her life, "The Miracle Worker," was a tremendous hit in the late 1950s.

By 1960 and Helen's eightieth birthday, her health began to fail. Yet she made the remarkable announcement that, "I will always—as long as I have breath—work for the handicapped."[18] In 1963 John F. Kennedy conferred upon her the Presidential Medal of Freedom. Suffering from a series of strokes, Helen made fewer and fewer appearances as she became unable to communicate or think clearly. In 1968 she died at her home in Westport, Connecticut.

Books by Helen Keller:
The Story of My Life (1902)
Optimism (1903)
The World I Live In (1908)
Song of the Stone Wall (1910)
Out of the Dark (1913)
My Religion (1927)
Midstream (1929)
We Bereaved (1929)
Peace at Eventide (1932)
Helen Keller's Journal (1938)
Let Us Have Faith (1940)
Teacher: Annie Sullivan Macy (1955)
The Open Door (1957)

Endnotes

1. Tames, Richard. *Helen Keller* (London: Franklin Watts, 1989), p. 10.
2. McHenry, Robert, ed. *Famous American Women* (New York: Dover Publications, Inc., 1980), p. 222.
3. Tames, p. 15.
4. Lash, Joseph P., *Helen and Teacher: The Story of*

Helen Keller and Anne Sullivan Macy (New York: Delacorte Press, 1980), p. 776.

5. Ibid., p. 776.
6. Ibid., p. 780.
7. Ibid., p. 781.
8. Ibid., p. 270.
9. Ibid., p. 786.
10. Ibid., p. 191.
11. Brown, p. 78.
12. Lash, p. 240.
13. Cullen-DuPont, Kathryn. *The Encyclopedia of Women's History in America* (New York: Facts On File, Inc., 1996), p. 110.
14. Tames, p. 24.
15. Ibid., p. 29.
16. Ibid., p. 26.
17. Ibid.
18. Ibid., p. 29.

R EBECCA
L UKENS

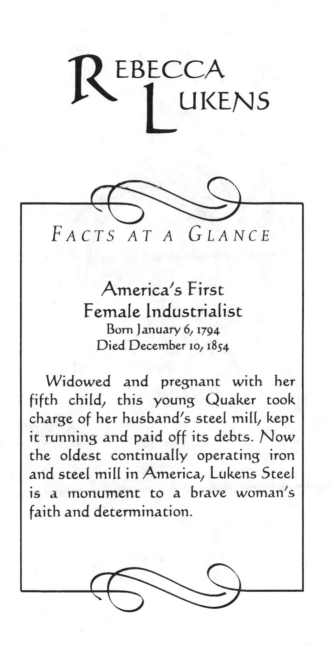

FACTS AT A GLANCE

**America's First
Female Industrialist**
Born January 6, 1794
Died December 10, 1854

Widowed and pregnant with her fifth child, this young Quaker took charge of her husband's steel mill, kept it running and paid off its debts. Now the oldest continually operating iron and steel mill in America, Lukens Steel is a monument to a brave woman's faith and determination.

R EBECCA L UKENS

In the summer of 1825 Charles Lukens died of a sudden illness. His thirty-one-year-old wife, Rebecca, pregnant with their fifth child, wondered how she would manage. They had been so close; she had depended on him so much. Rebecca struggled not to think of what life would be like without him as heaviness filled her chest.

Added to everything else, the mill was deeply in debt. Rebecca knew nothing about running a business, but that's exactly what her husband had in mind when he spoke his last words to her. In her memoirs she recalled, "My husband had just commenced the Boiler Plate Business and secured sufficient workmen to carry it on. This was a new branch in Pennsylvania and he was sanguine in his hopes of success. It was his dying request that he wished me to continue and I promised to comply."

A female ironmaster! It was unheard of, ludi-
crous. Yet that's what Charles Lukens wanted
Rebecca to do, and for her there was no possibility of going back on her word. She was a devout Christian who had made a promise.

When word spread to the mill's workers of
Charles Lukens' death, they paid their respects
to the man they had come to admire deeply.
Then with resignation and sadness they packed
up their families and headed to Pittsburgh to
find new jobs.

Rebecca heard about their plans and acted
quickly. Without these men, the mill would go
under. She hurried out in her carriage, inter-
cepting the workers as they headed toward the
main road.

"Please stay with us," urged the young
widow.

Although they liked her well enough, the
men hardened themselves. After all, no one
lives on sentiment.

Then she dropped the bombshell. "I am going to run the mill," Rebecca told the wide-
eyed workers. "My husband asked me to do so
before he died."

The men were incredulous. "No woman can
run a steel mill," they told her flatly. They
hated being so blunt considering her condition,
but this woman had to face reality. Iron-smelt-
ing and steel-making were men's work. Still,
there was something so winsome about Rebecca that they stopped long enough to listen.

She continued, refusing to sugarcoat her plea.

"Making a success of the mill will be difficult," Rebecca explained, "but if you stay with me, I will take care of you."

The men scratched their heads as they consulted their wives and each other. It wasn't like they wanted to leave the beautiful Chester County, Pennsylvania countryside or turn their backs on Rebecca Lukens. But could she pull it off? Persuaded by Rebecca's clear-headed realism and determination, the men returned to their jobs.

As she assumed the duties of "iron mistress," Rebecca Lukens was not without her critics. Most people believed that a steel mill was no place for a woman, especially a pregnant Quaker. But what else could she do? There seemed no other way to keep her family going. Besides, Rebecca had made a solemn promise to her husband, and promises had to be kept.

Her men rallied around her, though. They were especially grateful that unlike other steel mills, work did not stop when the nearby river ran too low to continue production. Rather than lay off her workers, Rebecca employed them on the adjoining farm.

In nine years the debts were paid off. Rebecca also steered the company through six financial panics. Through it all, her employees never spent a day out of work.

In addition, Rebecca was forward-looking like her husband had been, interested in the march of technological progress. She "prophesied" that one day there would be a high bridge spanning the Brandywine creek, instead of the small stone bridges in use at the time. Such a superstructure would permit trains to come closer to her iron and steel works. Then her product could be sent further than the fifty to seventy-five miles it had reached before that. In 1833 the bridge became reality, and Lukens Steel's business contacts expanded greatly.

Lukens Steel is now the oldest continually operating iron and steel mill in America. Robert Wolcott, past president of the company and her descendant, cited her

> simple directness, faith, sincerity, and earnestness. . . . These indeed were contributions, rockbedded in the eternal and priceless values of character. She had known what suffering is, and out of that suffering arose strength and understanding and determination.[1]

America's first woman industrialist was born near the Brandywine area of Pennsylvania in 1794. She was the oldest child of Isaac and Martha Pennock, prosperous Quakers. While Rebecca's father had been a farmer, he turned to iron-making in 1793. This was just after the American Revolution, and the British no longer could forbid the "colonists" to produce their own iron.

Isaac owned and operated the Federal Slitting Mill on Buck Run in Chester County. In 1810 he hooked up with the enterprising Quaker Jesse Kersey, founder of Coatesville, Pennsylvania as well as the Brandywine Iron Works and Nail Factory. Isaac Pennock became the sole owner of the enterprise in 1817.

Rebecca's youth focused on the mill, church activities and farming the land on which her family lived. She especially loved horseback riding, animal husbandry and reading, particularly Shakespeare. The young Quaker had many friends.

As a child she also enjoyed visiting her father at the mill. Rebecca was intrigued by the mechanics of making iron and steel. In addition, she was proud of the way her father took a special interest in each of his men.

Rebecca married Charles Lukens, a physician from Philadelphia, when she was eighteen. Lukens left his practice to pursue his new family's iron-making business. Isaac Pennock leased him the mill for $420 a year, making him a junior partner. The one condition was that upon Isaac Pennock's death, Rebecca would inherit the mill.

Charles Lukens was a visionary, a man who wanted to go beyond making just iron rods and nails. Soon he began producing iron plates for trains and steamships. In 1818 when the *S.S. Codorus* was the first American ship to use steel plates, they were of his creation. Lukens Steel gained a reputation for excellence in making "quality boilerplates." Unfortunately, the ironmaster had just twelve years to enjoy his new enterprise, young wife and family.

After Luken's death, Rebecca struggled to regain her equilibrium. Her faith and determination led her back to wholeness. Later she would write an autobiography for her children in which she shared what that period of mourning and its challenges had been like for her.

Describing her marriage as "those few brief years of bliss," Rebecca cautioned her children against making "this earth their idol." Their focus in life should be worship of their Creator. Rebecca wrote, "In bitter sorrow have I learned this lesson and fain would I guard you my beloved girls from the fatal error."[2]

Not only her children benefited from Rebecca Lukens's wisdom. Robert Wolcott praised her as a devout Christian whose "kindliness . . . bound to her in affectionate esteem the men who worked in this Iron Industry which she directed."[3]

Her son-in-law Charles Huston took over the iron and steel works in 1849, but Rebecca remained a very present help and guide until her death on December 10, 1854. Robert Wolcott

called her an "Ironmaster and Christian, [who]
contributed to the development of American
Industry at its best . . ."[4]

Her story was so inspiring that during the
1950s a radio drama captured it for a large
audience, with Helen Hayes playing the part of
Rebecca Lukens.

Endnotes

1. "A Woman in Steel," by Robert W. Wolcott. A New-
   comen Address, 1940, pp. 24-25.
2. Ibid., p. 19.
3. Ibid., p. 18.
4. Ibid, p. 25.

Bibliography

Martinez, Julia C. "Paying Honor to a Woman
    of Steel," *Philadelphia Inquirer*, January 6,
    1994.

DOLLEY MADISON

FACTS AT A GLANCE

"The Queen of
Washington City"
Born May 20, 1768
Died July 12, 1849

A lively and sociable first lady, she served as official hostess for both the Jefferson and Madison administrations. When the British burned the White House during the War of 1812, she showed great heroism in rescuing important state documents and artifacts before they could be destroyed by the enemy. Later she was instrumental in the Washington City reconstruction effort.

DOLLEY MADISON

Washington D.C.'s first restaurant opened in the autumn of 1802, and the Secretary of State's wife, the vivacious Dolley Madison, insisted on dining there. She didn't realize that the Oyster House catered to men and that, according to rumor, the only female patrons were prostitutes from Baltimore. Her husband, James Madison, didn't have the heart to disappoint his wife, however, so he sent one of his clerks to the restaurant to make reservations for him and Dolley for the next night.

The owner was a bit startled by the booking, and he rushed to clean up the place before the Madisons' arrival. The Oyster House sparkled by the time Dolley got there. In place of rough debates and questionable "business transactions," the other diners spoke in a low, conversational manner. Nor were there any Baltimore streetwalkers around. Dolley thoroughly enjoyed her oysters and told the proprietor she would be coming back for more.

She was such a social powerhouse that when respectable Washingtonians found out she had gone there to eat, they began patronizing the Oyster House immediately. The clientele changed overnight. Two new taverns opened to accommodate the raucous customers who were left behind.

On May 20, 1768 Dorothea Payne was born in Guilford County, North Carolina. She moved with her family to a plantation in Hanover County, Virginia as an infant. Her little brother, William, called her "Dolley" as they were growing up, and the name stuck. John and Mary Payne were Quakers, and when Dolley was fifteen, they sold their land and freed their slaves, then settled in Philadelphia. The Quakers were the first religious group in America to come out strongly against slavery.

Dolley was tutored at home and educated for a time in a Quaker school in Virginia. As a member of the Society of Friends, she was taught to be reserved in manner and speech, as well as to avoid ostentation. Dolley, however, had difficulty conforming to this ideal. Full of energy, she enjoyed playing competitively with

her brothers. In addition, her maternal Grandmother Cole, an Anglican, taught her to appreciate pretty clothes and fine food. Once her
grandmother gave Dolley a gold pin, and since
it was frowned upon by her religion to display
jewelry, the girl wore it under her dress.

In Philadelphia John Payne tried to earn a
living manufacturing laundry starch, but the
business went under. He lived almost like a
hermit afterward, and Dolley and her mother
began taking in boarders to pay the bills. One
of their guests was New York State Senator
Aaron Burr, who made romantic overtures toward the highly attractive Dolley. But Burr was
married, so Dolley rejected his attentions,
choosing instead John Todd, Jr., a Quaker attorney whom she wed in January of 1790. They
had two sons. When a yellow fever epidemic
tore through Philadelphia three years later,
Dolley's husband and first son died.

Aaron Burr watched after the beautiful
widow, concerned for her welfare. He introduced Dolley to the solid, upstanding Con-
gressman James Madison of Virginia. Dolley
wasn't sure about him at first, perhaps because
they were seventeen years apart in age, but she
quickly overcame her reservations and they
married on September 15, 1794. Theirs was a
happy union of opposites. Madison was quiet,
pensive and slightly built, while his extroverted
and physically robust wife thrived on social
gatherings. The couple had no children. Early

in her marriage Dolley Madison became an Episcopalian, finding that expression of the Christian faith better suited to her than the austerity and reticence of the Quakers.

The Madisons resided from 1797 until 1801 at his Montpelier estate in Orange County, Virginia near Thomas Jefferson's Monticello. Jefferson was elected president in 1800, and he made Madison his Secretary of State. In Washington, the nation's new capital, Dolley became the center of the city's social life, gaining the nickname "Queen of Washington City."

She also served the administration in an unusual capacity. Since Jefferson was a widower, he needed an official hostess, a post that perfectly suited Mrs. Madison. Dolley became first lady in her own right when her husband won the election of 1808. Her cheerful and gregarious personality helped her husband politically because his style was so bland. She often made campaign appearances with him, and Madison became far more outgoing and personally attractive to voters while in his wife's company. His presidential opponent, Charles Cotesworth Pinckney, remarked, "I was beaten by Mr. and Mrs. Madison. I might have had a better chance had I faced Mr. Madison alone."[1]

During James Madison's presidency, strong party factionalism developed, creating bitter undertones in American politics. The first lady's genuine friendliness went far in soothing ruffled feathers. She included members of opposing contingents at her social functions, treating both in her signature friendly way.

John Tyler's first wife said that Dolley Madison "added a new dimension to Washington society." She was the center of everything fashionable in the nation's capital.[2] American women came to judge trends and styles according to what Dolley wore, ate and said. Although she was widely celebrated and adored, she never became a snob. In fact, the wife of the British Minister to the United States loathed the first lady for including common people among her guests.

In August 1814 America was at war with the British, whose troops advanced toward Washington with the objective of burning it down. Before President Madison rode off to the front to inspect his army, he urged his wife to return to Montpelier. She refused to budge, however, until she was sure of his safety. At lunch time on the 24th Dolley heard cannon fire and set about to commandeer a large wagon in which she loaded the White House's silver and china, along with books and important state documents.

Volunteers in the effort urged her to leave when they learned the quickness of the British advance, but Dolley went back in one last time to save a Gilbert Stuart painting of George Washington. People lavishly praised her heroism, but Dolley responded, "Anyone would have done what I did."[3]

After the war, the president's residence was repaired, along with other buildings the British had destroyed, and Dolley Madison was at the forefront of the effort. She told one woman, "We shall rebuild Washington City. The enemy cannot frighten a free people."[4] During the reconstruction, the Madisons moved between two different homes in Washington.

James Madison served for two terms, then retired to Montpelier where he and Dolley entertained frequently. After his visit in 1824, the Marquis de Lafayette remarked, "Nowhere have I encountered a lady who is lovelier or more steadfast."[5]

As the former president's health declined, Dolley frequently read to him and acted as his secretary. She wrote down his final address to the nation shortly before his death in 1836.

Dolley went to live in Washington so she could remain active in its social circles. She was stretched financially, though, due to her playboy son Payne Todd's gambling debts. Dolley sold Montpelier to pay off Payne's debts and to save him from prison. The loss of her home and her financial condition cut her entertaining down to one monthly event. Finally, Congress came to her aid by purchasing her husband's papers and setting up a trust fund for her as a former first lady. Throughout her difficult times she remained ebullient and warmhearted, dazzling her guests. President Martin Van Buren said of her, "Mrs. Madison is the most brilliant hostess this country has ever known."[6]

She died in Washington on July 12, 1849 at eighty-one.

Endnotes

1. Boller, Paul L., Jr. *Presidential Wives: An Anecdotal History* (New York: Oxford University Press, 1988), p. 38.
2. Ibid., p. 36.
3. Ibid., p. 43.
4. Ibid.
5. Ibid.
6. Ibid.

CATHERINE MARSHALL

FACTS AT A GLANCE

Inspirational Author
Born 1914
Died March 18, 1983

Raised in a poor Southern preacher's home, she found herself thrust into Washington, D.C. society as the young bride of a prominent pastor, who later became chaplain of the U.S. Senate. When he died at an early age, she began a writing career to support herself. The result was nineteen books and multiple millions in sales. Her writings emphasize faith in adversity and an intimate relationship with God.

CATHERINE MARSHALL

On a Sunday morning in the spring of 1946 Catherine Marshall gazed in concern at her husband Peter, pastor of New York Avenue Presbyterian Church in Washington, D.C. Normally strapping and ruddy, today he looked drawn and gray. The demands of Peter Marshall's large congregation, besides countless nationwide appearances and speeches, had worn him out.

As Peter stepped into the pulpit to begin his sermon, Catherine whispered a prayer for him. The tall preacher launched into his message, but without his usual gusto. A few minutes later he muttered, "I'm terribly sorry, but I cannot go on." Suddenly he grasped the pulpit, then staggered backward.

Catherine rushed to his side, committing her young son, Peter John, to the care of a close friend. At the hospital she learned that her husband had suffered a massive heart attack. The doctors told her and Peter flatly that unless he modified his reckless schedule, he would not live much longer.

Following a restless convalescence, Peter returned to work with typical zeal. In 1947 he accepted the chaplaincy of the United States Senate. Although Catherine pleaded with her husband to take it easier, Peter seemed no more capable of slowing down than a robin can keep from appearing in early spring.

On the morning of January 25, 1949 Catherine became a widow at the age of thirty-four. She had never held a full-time job and had just recently recovered from a two-year battle with tuberculosis. Her future appeared stark and unpromising.

─────❦─────

Sarah Catherine Wood was born in Greenville, Tennessee in 1914, the first of John and Leonora (Whitaker) Wood's three children. Her father was a Presbyterian minister, and Catherine moved several times during her youth as he served parishes in Florida, Mississippi and West Virginia. In her book, *Meeting God at Every Turn*, Catherine described her childhood as secure and happy in spite of the economic constraints her family knew during the Depression of the 1930s. John Wood's salary came directly from the offering plate, which didn't usually brim over in those years.

Keeping his office at home so that he could be near his children, Wood was a constant presence in Catherine's young life. Although he was strict, Wood was humble and had a good sense of humor. Catherine recalled when he visited a new member of the church, a manual laborer with the railroad. The man was so grimy that he wouldn't shake the pastor's hand. Wood knelt down and rubbed his hands in the coal dust so they could meet as equals.

Catherine's mother, Leonora, is best remembered as the heroine on whose early life the book and TV show *Christy* were based. She carried her high spirits from the impoverished mountains of Tennessee, where she had taught in a mission school, to her home and family. Catherine remembered the way her mother had of making her children feel financially secure. In spite of Catherine's frequently patched clothes and meals of french fries, biscuits and gravy, and fried mush, she felt confident as her mother proclaimed that God would always provide their needs. Leonora Wood often sent meals to the sick and those in worse economic straits than herself. She also helped establish a community center for the poor, where she taught classes in child-rearing, crafts, health care and the Bible.

During her adolescence, Catherine decided there were three things she wanted in life: to be a writer; to attend Agnes Scott College, a private girl's school near Atlanta, Georgia; and to marry a wonderful man. Although Agnes Scott accepted her, Catherine feared that she could not go. In *Meeting God at Every Turn*, she recalled:

> By the time I graduated from high school the depression was daily dealing our town devastating blows: businesses failing, banks closing, bankruptcies, suicides, almost everyone living on credit. With our family's hand-to-mouth existence, how could there possibly be any money for college?[1]

Just as Catherine decided she could not in good conscience ask her family to fund her education, her mother encouraged her to draw on God's endless resources. Catherine learned from that experience that when God puts a dream in someone's heart, He brings it to pass.

One night she and her mother knelt by the guest room bed and turned the problem of college tuition over to God.

> Several days later Dad and Mother decided that by faith, I should go ahead and make preparations for Agnes Scott. They felt strongly that this was right and that the Lord would soon confirm it. I was not

so sure. . . . Days passed, then weeks.
Then one day Mother opened a letter and
gave a whoop of joy. . . . [It] contained an
offer from a special project of the federal
government for Mother to write the history of the county. With what I already
had [saved], her salary would be more
than enough for my college expenses.[2]

Catherine realized the second part of her
youthful dreams—marriage—at Agnes Scott.
While a freshman she heard a young Scottish
immigrant named Peter Marshall preach at Atlanta's Westminster Presbyterian Church. He
was humorous and handsome, with a fresh approach to Christianity. People who heard him
preach said that Marshall always made God
more approachable. He often spoke of God as
accessible and warm, rather than demanding
and distant. Marshall drew large numbers of
the Atlanta area's college students to his services, including Catherine Wood, who found
the single pastor "enchanting."
The moonstruck college girl filled journal after journal bemoaning her inability to make the
celebrated minister notice her. By her junior
year, she decided the quest was impossible and
made up her mind to get over him. At the
same time, however, Peter Marshall began
seeking her company. Catherine accepted the
popular clergyman's proposal at the end of her
senior year. Her father performed their mar-

riage ceremony on November 4, 1936 in Keyser, West Virginia.

For the next two years the celebrated New York Avenue Presbyterian Church in the nation's capital kept asking Peter to be its pastor. When he finally accepted, Marshall and his bride moved to Washington. At age twenty-three Catherine became "hostess to a steady stream of social functions in one of Washington's largest downtown churches."[3] For the time being, her dream of becoming a writer would have to wait.

On January 21, 1940 Catherine bore a son, Peter John Marshall, making her young life even more complete. Disaster struck, however, three years later when Catherine discovered she had tuberculosis and was ordered to bed. Peter encouraged her during the lonely, discouraging times, saying that someday she would be grateful for the experience. At the time, though, she had difficulty accepting that.

Catherine's recovery was a spiritual battleground. On it she learned many lessons that she would someday pass along to her readers, especially that God often demonstrates His power when humans are at their most helpless. She wrote:

> [F]or me this became a period of equipping—of spiritual preparation—for a tumultuous life of changes, of great, high moments to follow and plunging low

points. From the vantage point of the
years, I can see now that my being forced
to lie down in the green pastures beside
very still waters indeed—the isolation of
our bedroom—was a time of training.
Day by day God was the Teacher and I,
the pupil.[4]

The intimate relationship that she developed
with God not only took Catherine Marshall
through the crisis of her illness, it also sustained her through the dark valley of her husband's death in 1949. In addition the lessons
she learned helped make her one of America's
most beloved authors.

Not long after Peter's death, Catherine's financial advisors forecast deep gloom. They suggested she sell the family car and the Marshalls'
vacation home on Cape Cod. She decided to
wait for God's answer to her money crunch.
Shortly afterward a publishing house approached
her. Would she put together a book of her husband's best-loved sermons? Catherine felt that
the project might represent the fulfillment of her
girlhood dream of writing. In addition to editing
Marshall's sermons, Catherine asked if she could
write an introduction to the book. At first her
editor merely humored her, but when he saw the
depth and vibrancy of her writing, he enthusiastically agreed to use it.

Mr. Jones, Meet the Master became a runaway
bestseller. Soon there were plans for Catherine

to write Peter's life story. Released in 1951, *A Man Called Peter* has sold over four million copies to date and was a major motion picture.

Catherine's success as an author was assured. Through candid writing in which she not only discussed how God constantly showed His love in her life but also revealed her many flaws, Catherine drew millions of readers. They believed that if she could overcome her weaknesses, surmount life's trials and experience God's presence, so could they. Like her husband, Catherine's frank style invited people to develop intimacy with God.

In 1959 Catherine married former *Guideposts* editor Leonard LeSourd, who had three children from a previous marriage. Together they collaborated on many writing projects and began a publishing venture called Chosen Books. They also started a national intercessory prayer organization.

In her life Catherine Marshall published nineteen books, with *Christy* being the most successful commercially. After its release in 1967, the novel spent thirty-nine weeks on the *New York Times* bestseller list. It has sold eight million copies in its ninety printings. The popular author died on March 18, 1983 after a long illness.

Other books by Catherine Marshall:
To Live Again (1957)
Beyond Ourselves (1961)

Something More (1974)
Adventures in Prayer (1975)
The Helper (1978)
My Personal Prayer Diary (1979)
Julie (1984)
Friends with God (1956)
God Loves You (1953)
Catherine Marshall's Story Bible (1982)
The Prayers of Peter Marshall (1949)
Let's Keep Christmas (1952)
The First Easter (1959)
John Doe, Disciple (now entitled *Heaven Can Wait*) (1963)
The Best of Peter Marshall (1983)
A Closer Walk (1986)
Light in My Darkest Night (1989)
Mr. Jones, Meet the Master (1949)
A Man Called Peter (1951)
To Live Again (1957)
Meeting God at Every Turn (1980)

Endnotes

1. Marshall, Catherine. *Meeting God at Every Turn* (Carmel, NY: Guideposts, 1980), p. 44.
2. *Ibid.*, p. 46.
3. *Ibid.*, p. 83.
4. *Ibid.*, p. 86.

PHOEBE WORRALL PALMER

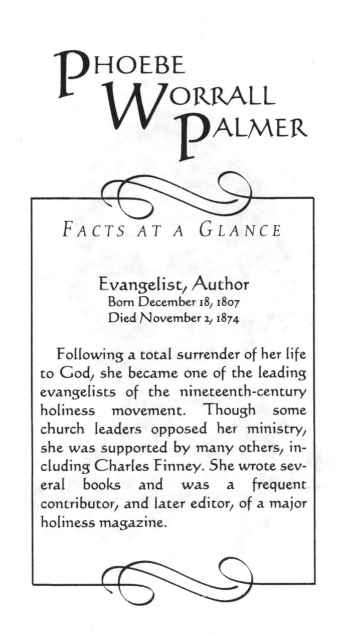

FACTS AT A GLANCE

Evangelist, Author
Born December 18, 1807
Died November 2, 1874

Following a total surrender of her life to God, she became one of the leading evangelists of the nineteenth-century holiness movement. Though some church leaders opposed her ministry, she was supported by many others, including Charles Finney. She wrote several books and was a frequent contributor, and later editor, of a major holiness magazine.

PHOEBE WORRALL PALMER

T he young woman was distraught as she faced Phoebe Palmer at the back of the tent following a moving revival meeting. "Thank you for taking the time to talk to me," the earnest lady began. "I know that you will understand how I feel."

Mrs. Palmer regarded her kindly. "What is it, child? What is weighing you down so much?"

The woman fidgeted with her necklace as she spoke. "God has called me to lead public meetings so others can come to Christ, but my church has reprimanded me for doing so. I want its blessing, but I also want to preach. How can I go against God?" she pleaded.

"You cannot," Phoebe Palmer stated. "Many church people persist in thinking that it is unbiblical for women to take leadership positions, to pray and prophesy in public. But it is indeed unbiblical for man to refuse what God directs."

"Then you are sure God has called me?"

"Child, if *you* are certain, you have heard His voice clearly."

"I am sure that I have," she insisted. "It's just that sometimes, when pressures fill me from the outside, I doubt." She hesitated. "Do you ever face opposition?"

The delightful woman evangelist laughed softly. "My goodness, yes! All the time! But I persist because this is what God has called me to do."

———✦———

One of the nineteenth century's preeminent evangelists, Phoebe Worrall was born in New York City a week before Christmas in 1807. She was the fourth of Henry Worrall and Dorothea Wade Worrall's ten children. Mr. Worrall, owner of an iron foundry and machine shop, had come to America from England. As a young boy he was converted at a meeting led by John Wesley. He emigrated to the U.S. in search of greater religious and political freedom. He and his American wife were Methodists and raised their children accordingly, observing daily family worship.

Phoebe began writing poetry at the age of ten as well as keeping a diary. In it she spoke of her love for her parents and admiration for Methodist ministers.[1] Although she did not marry one of those pastors, at nineteen she

wed a fellow Methodist, Walter C. Palmer. He
was a homeopathic physician who had been
"powerfully converted" at the age of thirteen.[2]
Both had a passion for sharing the gospel of Jesus Christ and became active in the holiness
revivals of the 1830s. The Palmers had six children, three of whom died shortly after their
births.

In 1832 the Palmers went forward at a New
York revival to dedicate themselves to "the
work of spiritual holiness."[3] The pursuit of holiness deepened for Phoebe in 1837 when she
began to seek "entire sanctification":

> The Lord gave me such a view of my ut-
> ter pollution and helplessness, apart from
> the cleansing, energizing influences of the
> purifying blood of Jesus, and the quicken-
> ing aids of the Holy Spirit, that I have
> ever since retained a vivid realization of
> the fact.[4]

She and her sister Sarah started a women's
"Tuesday Meeting for the Promotion of Holiness" in 1835, and it lasted for over sixty years.
Those gatherings, consisting of Bible reading,
singing, prayer and personal testimonies, became a center for the holiness movement, in
which participants sought perfection in their
spiritual lives. Phoebe began discipling many
Christians, including two Methodist bishops,
Leonidas L. Hamline and Edmund S. Janes.

John Dempster, who founded Concord and Garrett Seminaries, also came under her influence. Many laypeople and pastors from other denominations attended as well. The Tuesday meetings became so big that eventually the Palmers' home could not accommodate everyone, and they moved to a bigger venue.

Phoebe also became active in social causes in the 1840s, especially with the poor and prisoners. From 1847 until 1858 she served as corresponding secretary of the New York Female Assistance Society for the Relief and Religious Instruction of the Sick Poor. As director of the Methodist Ladies' Home Missionary Society, Mrs. Palmer helped to found the Five Points Mission in a New York slum.

A writer as well as a preacher, Phoebe Palmer was a regular contributor to the *Guide to Holiness* magazine. She also wrote several books including *The Way of Holiness* (1845), *Entire Devotion* (1845), *Faith and Its Effects* (1846), *Incidental Illustrations of the Economy of Salvation* (1852), *Promises of the Father* (1859) and *Pioneer Experiences* (1868).

In the 1850s Phoebe and Walter Palmer began to conduct yearly revivals on the East coast and in Canada, especially at camp meetings during the summer and fall. They resided in New York City during the spring and winter, where Dr. Palmer practiced medicine. According to Kari Torjesen Malcolm, "In 1857-58, she was a major force in the holiness revival which spread across the country."[5] Palmer was not, however, always welcomed as a female evangelist, and at times this pioneering woman faced emphatic opposition. She addressed her pain over this resistance in *The Promise of the Father*, a book inspired by a Christian woman whose church rebuked her for speaking publicly about Christ:

> The church in many ways is a sort of potter's field where the gifts of women, as so many strangers, are buried. How long, O Lord, how long before man shall roll away the stone that we may see a resurrection?[6]

Mrs. Palmer maintained that God the Father has poured out His Spirit on both His sons and daughters, according to the prophecy of Joel 2:28-29. She realized that often Christians cited Paul's injunction against women speaking in the church in Corinthians and interpreted his message thus:

> It was in reference to this (disorder in the Corinthian church) that Paul enjoins silence, and not in reference to the exercise of the gift of prophecy. . . . Surely it is evident that the irregularities here complained of were peculiar to the church of Corinth, and, in fact, we may presume, were not even applicable to other Chris-

tian churches of Paul's day, much less
Christian churches of the present day, as
no such disorders exist. O, the endless
weight of responsibility with which the
church is pressing herself earthward
through the depressing influences of this
error: How can she rise while the gifts of
three-fourths of her membership are sep-
ulchred in her midst?

> Daughters of Zion, from the dust
> Exalt thy fallen head;
> Again in thy Redeemer trust.
> He calls thee from the dead.[7]

Charles Finney, the great nineteenth century
evangleist, threw in his lot with Phoebe Palmer
in proclaiming that men and women be allowed to address mixed-sex meetings. He was
part of a large evangelical assembly that met in
1827 to debate the issue. "Because Finney refused to compromise his stand, the door remained open for women to use their gifts in
some of the churches that were touched by the
revivals of the nineteenth century."[8] Curiously,
many of the nineteenth century's leading femi-
nists were profoundly affected by the revivals
led by Charles Finney, including Elizabeth
Cady Stanton, Caroline Severance and Pauline
Kellogg Wright Davis. A Wesleyan church in
Seneca Falls, New York hosted the first
women's rights convention. According to Kari

Torjesen Malcolm, "Revival seemed to come hand in hand with concern for the rights of slaves and women."[9]

Nevertheless, Phoebe Palmer did not speak out for women's rights, shunning unnecessary public notoriety. She also remained publicly neutral on slavery, in keeping with the Methodist position of her colleagues in the 1850s.

Dr. and Mrs. Palmer led revivals in England from 1859 to 1863, drawing thousands of people. Among them was a pastor's wife, Catherine Mumford Booth, who helped establish the Salvation Army. One report recorded, "Thousands on thousands are born again, through listening to the appeals of the Doctor and his lady."[10] During that sojourn, Dr. Palmer also purchased the magazine *Guide to Holiness*, and his wife became the editor. Phoebe Palmer remained in that position until her death. When the evangelist couple returned to America, they went to Illinois to conduct more revival meetings. At one of them Frances Willard, leader of the Women's Christian Temperance Union, went forward in response to Phoebe's call for the "higher Christian life."[11]

Phoebe Palmer was also active in social reform work. Her accomplishments included visiting prisoners at New York's Tombs reformatory, serving as corresponding secretary of the New York Female Assistance Society for the Relief and Religious Instruction of the Sick Poor, and founding the Five Points Mission in a sordid community. It offered twenty rent-free apartments, a chapel a classroom and baths.

In spite of her renown, Phoebe Palmer avoided publicity, to the extent that for years she did not allow her name to be printed on the title pages of her books.

Four Years in the Old World, a book she wrote in 1865, described the revivals she and her husband had led in Great Britain. Two years later they helped organize the National Association for the Promotion of Holiness, under whose auspices they conducted their evangelistic work.

Phoebe Palmer died at sixty-six on November 2, 1874, probably of pneumonia. At her funeral the Rev. T. DeWitt Talmadge credited her with leading 25,000 people to Christ. Shortly after Phoebe's death, her husband and her sister, Sarah Lankford, were married.

Endnotes

1. McCutcheon, W.J., essay in James, et al., eds. *Notable American Women* (Cambridge: Belknap Press, 1971), p. 13.
2. Ibid., p. 13.
3. Ibid.
4. Malcolm, Kari Torjesen. *Women at the Crossroads* (Downers Grove: InterVarsity Press, 1982), p. 119.
5. Ibid., p. 120.
6. Ibid.
7. Ibid., pp. 120-121.

8. Ibid., p. 121.
9. Ibid., p. 123.
10. McCutcheon, p. 13.
11. Malcolm, p. 123.

Bibliography

McHenry, Robert, ed. *Famous American Women* (New York: Dover Publications, Inc., 1980).

Rosa Parks

FACTS AT A GLANCE

"Mother of the
Civil Rights Movement"
Born February 4, 1913

Jailed for refusing to give up her bus seat to a white man, this African-American seamstress was propelled into the national spotlight when her arrest sparked a landmark civil rights case. But few realize that her quiet courage that day was an outgrowth of a lifelong walk of faith and principle.

R OSA P ARKS

At quitting time on Thursday, December 1, 1955 Rosa Parks wearily left the Montgomery Fair department store. She was glad to have the long working day behind her. The forty-two-year-old seamstress sometimes operated a large commercial steam press. She was not physically sturdy, though, and that night every muscle seemed to ache as she walked a half-block to the Court Square bus stop. The first vehicle so bulged with passengers that Parks decided to wait for the next one. She couldn't bear the thought of standing all the way home after her grueling day. Knowing that it would be a few minutes, she stepped into a drugstore to do some quick Christmas shopping, then rejoined the crowd at the bus stop.

Soon another hulking city bus swung to the curb with the familiar whine of its brakes.

Parks saw to her relief that there were many vacant seats. She willed her aching feet up the accordion-like stairs and dropped her dime into the fare box. As it clinked to the bottom, she recognized the harsh profile of the white driver, J.F. Blake. Twelve years earlier he had kicked her off his bus for refusing to re-enter it from the rear where blacks sat. She had consistently avoided getting on his bus since then, but tonight Parks felt too tired to wait for another. Blake didn't seem to remember her, nor did he require the black riders to board from the rear that night.

As the bus idled loudly, Parks made her way down the aisle past the first ten rows, reserved for whites. Twenty-six more beyond them were for blacks, who made up most of the city's bus riders. Nevertheless, the drivers had the legal right to order blacks to give up their seats for whites any time they pleased.

Parks lowered herself onto a shiny vinyl seat, and the bus took off with its customary lurch. Several stops later a white man boarded. Finding the white section filled, bus driver Blake issued an order. Swinging around in his tall seat, he pointed toward the black section. "You let him have those front seats," he directed.

Although the white man only required one seat, Blake didn't want him to suffer the indignity of sitting next to any blacks.

No one moved. Blake was not pleased.

"You all better make it light on yourselves and let me have those seats," he hissed as he steered the bus down the street.

With the rolling of eyes and shuffling of unhappy feet, three blacks abandoned their seats. They didn't want any trouble. They just wanted to go home. Only Rosa Parks sat still. She had been deferring to white people all her life. Now something inside told her "no more." Besides, she reasoned, why should a woman—any woman—give up her seat for a man? Although she was frightened of the consequences, Rosa was too tired physically and emotionally to stand the rest of the way home.

Blake pulled over to the curb, then stormed down the aisle like a self-contained tornado. He planted his feet in front of the seamstress. "Look, woman, I told you I wanted the seat. Are you going to stand up?"

Parks lifted her chin as she met his glowering eyes. "No," she responded calmly.

"If you don't stand up," Blake threatened, "I'm going to have you arrested."

"Go ahead, you may do that," the petite woman answered.

Blake thundered off the bus and summoned police help on a pay phone. Sensing trouble, several blacks hurried off. Two officers arrived minutes later.

"That one won't stand up," the driver pointed at his defiant rider.

"Why haven't you obeyed the law?" asked one cop.

"I felt I shouldn't have to," Parks answered respectfully. "Why do you push us around?"

Her dignity and calmness were disconcerting. "I don't know, but the law is the law, and you're under arrest," he declared.

"Do you wish to press charges against her?" the senior officer asked Blake.

"I most certainly do," he retorted.

Only then did Rosa Parks leave her seat.

The policemen escorted her to the back seat of their patrol car and took her to Montgomery City Hall. The officers vainly tried to establish that Parks had defied the law due to drunkenness. Why else would she have challenged the very fabric of southern segregation?

A deputy sheriff fingerprinted and photographed her, then allowed Parks one phone call. He placed her in a cell while she waited for her husband Raymond to come. Parks was fined $10 and an old friend, a white attorney named Clifford Durr, posted her bond for $100. He knew of Rosa's predicament through E.D. Nixon, former head of the Montgomery National Association for the Advancement of Colored People (NAACP), for which Parks had served as secretary. An eyewitness to her arrest had called Nixon about it right away.

In response to the Rosa Parks incident, Montgomery's black clergy took immediate action. Led by Dexter Avenue Baptist Church's pastor, Martin Luther King, Jr., a strike against the bus company was announced on December 5 under the auspices of the Montgomery Improvement Association (MIA). King wrote in his book, *Stride Toward Freedom:*

> [O]ne day after finishing school, I was called to a little church, down in Montgomery, Alabama. And I started preaching there. Things were going well in that church, it was a marvelous experience. But one day a year later, a lady by the name of Rosa Parks decided that she wasn't going to take it any longer. . . . It was the beginning of a movement.[1]

In 1954 the U.S. Supreme Court had ruled in *Brown vs. The Board of Education* that public school segregation was unconstitutional. Blacks throughout the South anticipated a new day as the legally recognized equals of whites. It quickly became obvious to those living in Montgomery, Alabama, however, that segregation still needed to be challenged on other levels. Rosa Parks provided an opportunity for just that. Its implications would spread far past the state of Alabama.

At first the MIA called for a modest change in the situation. They asked that blacks and whites be seated on a "first come, first served" basis, with blacks filling the back of the bus first. They also requested that the bus company hire black drivers and treat passengers of color courteously. Following the city's arrest of King and other boycott leaders, the Ku Klux Klan's bombing of King's house and the continual harassment of black motorists for the most trivial—and fabricated—traffic violations, however, the black community insisted on complete integration.

The bus strike lasted 382 days. During that time, both Rosa and Raymond Parks lost their jobs because of their involvement in it. The city's black community as a whole also endured enormous personal hardships. The boycott, however, did cripple the city's white-owned bus company financially as roughly ninety percent of Montgomery's blacks walked or carpooled to their destinations. Black churches donated Sunday offerings to help cover the expenses of transporting their brothers and sisters. Although some boycott participants advocated violence against their white oppressors, King insisted that Christian love overcome racial hatred.

On December 20, 1956 the municipal bus company relented when the Supreme Court deemed racial segregation on the buses unconstitutional.

———————<⊂≪≫⊃>———————

Rosa Lee McCauley was born in rural Alabama in 1913 to James and Leona McCauley.

Her father was a carpenter, and her mother taught elementary school—when there were jobs. Education for blacks was an after-thought in those days, and Leona often re-sorted to hairdressing and sewing to earn money.

The family moved to the Montgomery area during Rosa's childhood, but James was rest-less and left for months at a time to pursue building contracts in the north. When Rosa was five, her father left altogether. When her mother's parents came to their rescue, Rosa went to live on their farm near Montgomery. A former slave, Rosa's grandfather instilled in her that she was as good as any white.

When Rosa was eleven, her mother sent her to a Montgomery private school for black girls. Miss White's, also known as the Industrial School for Girls, was run by Alice L. White, a broad-minded New England activist. Although the expense severely strained family finances, Leona McCauley saw no other alternative. Rosa's first school had shut down due to a lack of funds.

Her grandfather's constant drilling about Rosa's equality to whites was reinforced at the new school. This sometimes deeply worried her grandmother. Once when Rosa refused to back down to a white bully, threatening him with a brick, her grandmother predicted that the little girl would be lynched by the time she was twenty-one. Throughout her childhood, Rosa

endured countless outrages against her because of her color, yet she believed strongly
that she, too, was created by God and had in-
nate worth and dignity.

During her tenth and eleventh grades, Rosa
took high school classes at the Alabama
Teacher's College for Negroes. She worked as
a seamstress in a factory as well as a housekeeper to pay for tuition. When her grandmother died and her mother became ill, Rosa
left school to work full-time and provide for the
family.

Times were hard during the Depression that
hit the nation in 1929, but Rosa worked cease-
lessly to keep the family farm from going under.
At eighteen she met a twenty-eight-year-old man
named Raymond Parks, a barber from
Montgomery. Due to the age difference and
Raymond's half-white, half-black parentage,
Rosa took a while to warm up to him. However,
his deep convictions about racial equality helped
win her over. In December 1932 they were married in a simple ceremony on the farm and went
to live in a Montgomery rooming house. A year
later Rosa finished her high school education, a
significant accomplishment for a black woman
then. Nevertheless, she could obtain only menial
work in a hospital and as a seamstress.

Throughout the 1940s and early '50s, Rosa
Parks served as secretary of the Montgomery
NAACP chapter, committed to enforcing vot-
ing rights for southern blacks and equal justice

under the law. A childless woman, she was especially committed to helping young black people gain entrance to colleges.

In 1954 E.D. Nixon introduced Rosa to attorney Clifford Durr and his wife Virginia. Clifford had served under President Harry Truman as director of the Federal Communications Commission. The Durrs were the first whites Rosa had ever met who were committed to civil rights. Virginia invited Rosa to join an integrated prayer group in her home. In the summer of 1955 she arranged a scholarship for Rosa so she could attend a seminar at the innovative Highlander Folk School in Monteagle, Tennessee. There Rosa learned about the nonviolent passive resistance of India's Mohandas Gandhi in his fight against British rule a decade earlier. The seminar was entitled "Racial Desegregation: Implementing the Supreme Court Decision."

Rosa Parks didn't know at the time that she stood on the brink of history.

E.D. Nixon had been waiting for the right moment to test the Montgomery and Alabama segregation laws. Two other women had been arrested in 1955 on city buses for noncompliance. Nixon, however, did not think he could build public opinion around them. One was a pregnant, unwed teen who had resisted arrest, and the other lived in a run-down shack with an alcoholic father. Neither was articulate. When he learned that Rosa Parks, his long-

time associate at the NAACP, had been arrested, Nixon moved quickly to seize the opportunity.

After enduring the bus incident, the continual torment by enemies of racial equality and
the subsequent Supreme Court decision in her
favor, Rosa Parks and her family moved to Detroit in 1957. She continued her work on behalf of civil rights, attending rallies and making
speeches. She also labored hard to improve the
lot of those living in poverty in Detroit, in spite
of her own financial troubles.

In 1965 Parks joined the staff of U.S. Representative John Conyers, where she served until
1988. In the mid-1970s, she lost her husband,
brother and mother to cancer. During the '80s
and '90s, Parks, the recipient of many humanitarian awards, continued her campaign against
racial discrimination. With the proceeds from
one prize, she formed the Rosa and Raymond
Parks Institute for Self-Development. Its goal
was to assist young people with job and life
skills, as well as to teach the history of the civil
rights movement.

Rosa Parks remains one of America's most
beloved women, a living symbol that Christian
love can triumph over racial hatred and prejudice. Martin Luther King, Jr. once said of her,
"Nobody can doubt the height of her character, nobody can doubt the depth of her Christian commitment and devotion to the
teachings of Jesus. . . ."[2]

Endnotes

1. Hull, Mary. *Rosa Parks: Civil Rights Leader* (Chelsea House Publishers, New York, 1994), p. 85, quoting from King's book.
2. Ibid., p. 74.

Bibliography

Halberstam, David. *The Fifties* (New York: Villard Books, 1993).

King, Martin Luther Jr. *Stride Toward Freedom* (New York: Harper, 1958).

MOLLY PITCHER

FACTS AT A GLANCE

Revolutionary War Heroine
Born October 13, 1754
Died January 22, 1832

Though her true name was Mary Ludwig Hays McCauley, she is better known as "Molly Pitcher" for her courageous act of carrying water to thirsty soldiers at the Battle of Monmouth. By manning the cannon after her husband dropped from heat exhaustion, she helped turn the tide of the battle, which ended in a British retreat.

(Illustration is an artist's rendition; no portraits are available.)

Molly Pitcher

olly Hays watched as her husband John marched off to do battle on that steamy June day in 1778. A sound like a violent thunderclap pierced her ears as other soldiers' wives hastened to safety far behind the lines. Molly lingered, however, and when a cannon boomed, she knew her husband, a sergeant, was at his post.

Although the patriots weren't about to succumb to the British, many of them faded fast in the 100-degree heat. Molly heard their cries for "Water! Water!" and realized that if the men were not soon refreshed, the Americans might lose the battle. *We can't lose this fight because our men don't have enough water,* she thought. Without considering her personal safety, Molly rushed to a nearby spring and filled her pail with cold, clear water. Then, hitching up her long, hot skirts, she dashed toward the front, praying she wasn't too late.

On the battlefield the acrid stench of gunpowder nearly overcame her, but she steadied herself, making trip after trip from the spring to the dehydrated soldiers. Their throats thick with dust, they opened their mouths like baby birds and drank greedily as Molly poured water into them, beginning with the most urgent cases. As she worked, the young woman tried to keep track of John while he repeatedly shoved a hot ramrod down the cannon's barrel. Only when he slumped over his cannon with heat exhaustion, did Molly abandon her trips to the spring.

She hurried to John's side, took a rag and plunged it into her last pail of water. For several minutes Molly applied the cold compress to his temples, then she helped him into the cannon's shade. Her husband's partner at the cannon gaped in amazement as Molly took up the ramrod John had dropped.

"Load!" she hollered.

"But—" the man stammered.

"Load!" Molly insisted.

When he did so, she thrust the ramrod down the barrel of the cannon. The gunpowder and ammunition fused in an explosive roar, sending black soot all over Molly's sticky clothes. She served as the regiment's cannoneer for the rest of the fight, in spite of fatigue and hands that burned from the blistering ramrod. The Battle of Monmouth ended in a British retreat. Molly, who gained the nickname "Molly Pitcher" that day, lay depleted at her husband's side. Finally a soldier lifted her in his arms and carried Molly to a bed of blankets so she could rest properly from her heroic labors.[1]

Mary Ludwig was born in Trenton, New Jersey in 1754, twenty-two years before the Declaration of Independence. Until she was fifteen, she lived on a small dairy farm with her German immigrant father, John George Ludwig, and her mother, who may have been a Dutch woman named Gretchen. It is likely that they were observant Lutherans like other settlers in that area; Mary later joined the Lutheran church as an adult. Mr. Ludwig, who was probably overburdened with taxes, hired his daughter out as a doctor's servant. The physician lived in Carlisle, Pennsylvania, near the frontier portion of the state.

While still a teenager and in Doctor William Irvine's service, Molly, as she was more commonly known, married John Casper Hays on July 24, 1769. They had at least one son, John L. Hays. Over the next few years, the young couple came to believe strongly in the struggle for independence from Great Britain.

When the Revolution broke out, John Hays served in the First Company of Pennsylvania Artillery, first under Thomas Proctor, then with the Seventh Pennsylvania Regiment. Molly followed the example of many other soldiers' wives in becoming a camp follower to be with her husband. Although General Washington sometimes expressed vexation with those women for distracting his troops, he also realized their value as they performed important and often thankless jobs, such as preparing meals, cleaning and mending clothes, and volunteering at military hospitals. It is highly likely that Molly Hays came under the influence of Martha Washington, especially at Monmouth, as the general's wife encouraged the soldiers' spouses to give all they could to the patriot cause.

Molly was a physically sturdy woman, although her contemporaries described her as short. They also noted that she was thick and strong, a woman of coarse appearance who chewed tobacco and sometimes used improper language. In spite of her roughness, however, Molly was known as a kind person, full of courage.

At the Battle of Monmouth, New Jersey on June 28, 1778, Molly Hays secured her place in American history by valiantly ignoring her safety to carry water to the hot artillerymen. From then on the soldiers affectionately called her "Moll of the Pitcher" or "Molly Pitcher." There is a similar story about another patriot woman, Margaret Corbin, who also served as a cannoneer in battle; in fact, the two are sometimes confused in popular history.

The British, who had been relaxing at Monmouth on their way to New York, retreated that night. Ten thousand men on each side had fought that day, with sixty-nine American fatalities and more than three times that many British. General Washington personally thanked Molly "Pitcher" Hays and recommended to Congress that she be commissioned a sergeant and given half-pay for life.

After independence, Molly and John lived quietly in Carlisle where she worked as a domestic, and John became a barber. He died in 1789, probably due to wounds he suffered during the war. Molly took up additional work cleaning the Carlisle courthouse to make ends meet. She later married John "George" McCauley, himself a war veteran, whose last name was frequently spelled "M'Kolly." He passed away around 1813.

In 1822 Molly Pitcher began to receive a $40-a-year pension by an act of the Pennsylvania assembly. The bill was originally designated "for the relief of Molly M'Kolly" as a widow of a revolutionary soldier. On February 21, 1822, however, the act was amended to honor her service in the cause directly. It read, "for the relief of Molly M'Kolly, for her services during the Revolutionary War."[2]

On January 22, 1832 Molly Pitcher died in Carlisle. The story of her heroism became legendary after her death, partially due to John Greenleaf Whittier's book, *Moll Pitcher*. During the nation's centennial in 1876, Pennsylvania raised a monument to her memory at her burial site in Carlisle's Old Graveyard. There is also a memorial to her near the Monmouth battle site.

Endnotes

1. Gleiter, Jan and Thompson, Kathleen. *Molly Pitcher* (Milwaukee: Raintree Publishers, 1987), pp. 4-22, 26-32.
2. Cullen-DuPont, Kathryn. *The Encyclopedia of Women's History in America* (New York: Facts on File, 1996), p. 127.

Bibliography

McHenry, Robert, ed. *Famous American Women* (New York: Dover Publications, Inc., 1980).

Stevenson, Augusta. *Molly Pitcher: Girl Patriot* (Chicago: Spencer Press, 1952).

POCAHONTAS

FACTS AT A GLANCE

Indian Princess
Born c. 1595
Died March 1617

After earning her place in history by her brave rescue of Captain John Smith, this pre-adolescent Indian maiden grew to young adulthood, married Jamestown settler John Rolfe and became a favorite of English royalty before her untimely death at the age of twenty-one.

POCAHONTAS

—⬦⬦⬦—

Two large stones were brought in and placed before Powhatan, and Smith was dragged up to them and his head was placed upon them, that his brains might be beaten out with clubs. The fatal weapons were already raised, and the stern executioners looked for the signal, which should bid them descend upon the victim's defenseless head. But the protecting shield of divine Providence was over him, and the arm of violence was arrested. Pocahontas, the King's favorite daughter—at that time a child of twelve or thirteen years of age—finding that her piteous entreaties to save the life of Smith were unavailing, rushed forward, clasped his head in her arms, and laid her own upon it, determined either to save his life, or share his fate. Her generous and heroic conduct touched her father's iron heart, and the life of the captive was spared. . . .

"The account of this beautiful and most touching scene, familiar as it is to every one, can hardly be read with unmoistened eyes. The incident is so dramatic and startling, that it seems to preserve the freshness of novelty amidst a thousand repetitions. We could almost as reasonably expect an angel to have come down from heaven, and rescued the captive, as that his deliverer should have sprung from the bosom of Powhatan's family. The universal sympathies of mankind and the best feelings of the human heart have redeemed this scene from the obscurity which, in the progress of time, gathers over all but the most important events. It has pointed a thousand morals and adorned a thousand tales. Innumerable bosoms have throbbed and are yet to throb with generous admiration for the daughter of a people, whom we have been too ready to underrate. Had we known nothing of her, but what is related of her in this incident, she would deserve the eternal gratitude of the inhabitants of this country; for the fate of the colony may be said to have hung upon the arms of Smith's executioners." (Jared Sparks, 1839)1

Pocahontas was born in the vicinity of Jamestown, Virginia to Wahunsonacock (better known as Powhatan), chief of thirty Tidewater-area tribes. Her given name was Matoaka; Pocahontas, her nickname, meant "frolicsome" or "my favorite daughter."

In 1607 the Jamestown colony sprang up, the first permanent English settlement in America. The eleven-or twelve-year-old Pocahontas became a frequent visitor to the fort. She was tomboyish and delightful, capturing the Englishmen's hearts. Pocahontas often took gifts of food to relieve their hunger when their supplies ran low.

The Indian princess also became a buffer between her people and the British. Some historians believe that Powhatan encouraged his daughter's relationships with the colonists to secure their support in his battles with other tribes. Pocahontas may have been responsible for making the Jamestown settlement workable by promoting positive relations between the English and her people. Captain John Smith wrote in his memoirs about an incident in which Pocahontas saved him from being killed, one that many think is a myth (Smith was, after all, a notorious storyteller). In a 1995 history textbook, however, four scholars maintain that Smith's resourcefulness kept Jamestown from going under and that recent scholarship points to the truthfulness of his memoirs.[2]

Although the story has been embellished considerably over the years, it likely did happen. The vibrant young Pocahontas may easily have had a passionate crush on the dashingly handsome Smith and resorted to dramatic means to preserve his life.

In 1609 Captain Smith returned to England, and Pocahontas' visits became fewer and further between. This may have been due to her reaching puberty, with Powhatan thinking it unwise for her to be around older men.

Captain Samuel Argall detained Pocahontas in the spring of 1613 as a kind of hostage. He wanted to use her to secure the release of English prisoners from some Tidewater Indians, as well as to establish a permanent peace with that tribe. The Englishmen treated Pocahontas well, and Powhatan experienced no alarm over the incident. During that period, the Indian princess became a Christian and took the name "Rebecca" at her baptism.

Another significant development in her life was when John Rolfe, a widower who introduced tobacco to Virginia from the West Indies, fell in love with Pocahontas and petitioned Governor Thomas Dale for permission to marry her. In the letter he explained his intention to marry:

> but for the good of this plantation, for the honour of our countrie, for the glory of God, for my owne salvation, and for the converting to the true knowledge of God

and Jesus Christ, an unbeleeving crea-
ture, namely Pokahuntas.[3]

Considering the marriage a wise political
move, Powhatan gave his consent. The couple
got married in April 1614.

Their union furthered peace between the
English settlers and the Indians. During the
pre-revolutionary period of American history,
there was much speculation about what the
country might have been like had more Euro-
peans followed Rolfe's example. Many problems and hostilities between the races, it was
thought, might have been averted with more
intermarriage. The English colonists, however,
had been warned by their leaders to maintain
their racial purity when they reached the New
World.

In 1616 the Rolfes had a son whom they
named Thomas. They left for England the following year to secure more support for English
colonization in the New World. When King
James I met Pocahontas in England, he was so
impressed with her—and so upset with Rolfe
for presuming to marry such a royal soul—that
he charged the Englishman with taking unfair
advantage of her during her captivity. When
the king heard the whole story of their ro-
mance, however, his anger abated. Pocahontas
also charmed Queen Anne and became a favorite of English high society. She attended
many important functions, had her portrait

done for an engraving and drummed up support for the Jamestown enterprise.

While making preparations to return to America in March 1617, Pocahontas became fatally ill with smallpox. She died at age twenty-one in Gravesend, Kent and was buried there. Powhatan died two years later, and his half brother Opechancanough decided the best way to deal with the English "intruders" was to kill them. At his prompting, a massacre claimed 347 colonists on Good Friday, March 22, 1622. John Rolfe was numbered among the dead. Thomas Rolfe, it is said, went on to become the forefather of Virginia's Randolph and Bollings families.[4]

Endnotes

1. Tilton, Robert S. *Pocahontas: The Evolution of an American Narrative* (New York: Cambridge University Press, 1994), p. xvi.
2. Divine, Robert A., et al. *America Past and Present* (New York: Harper Collins College Publishers, 1995), p. 36.
3. Tilton, p. 14.
4. Ibid., p. 45.

Bibliography

Sparks, Jared. "Lives of Alexander Wilson and Captain John Smith" in *The Library of American Biography, vol. 2* (Boston: Hilliard, Gray, 1839), pp. 239-241.

Betsy Ross

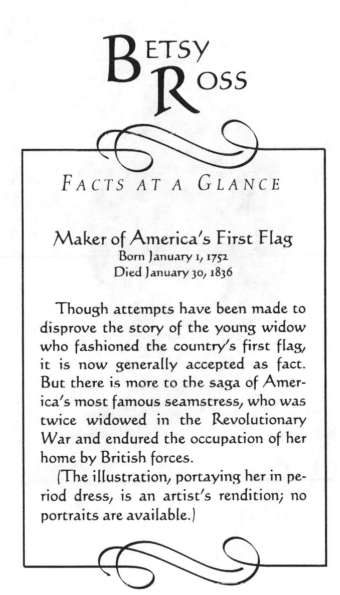

FACTS AT A GLANCE

Maker of America's First Flag
Born January 1, 1752
Died January 30, 1836

Though attempts have been made to disprove the story of the young widow who fashioned the country's first flag, it is now generally accepted as fact. But there is more to the saga of America's most famous seamstress, who was twice widowed in the Revolutionary War and endured the occupation of her home by British forces.

(The illustration, portaying her in period dress, is an artist's rendition; no portraits are available.)

B ETSY
R OSS

———⟨⫘⟩———

I remember to have heard my grand-mother, Elizabeth Claypoole (Betsy Ross), frequently narrate the circumstance of her having made the first Star-Spangled Banner; that it was a specimen flag made to the order of a Committee of Congress, acting in conjunction with General Washington who called upon her personally at her store in Arch Street, below Third Street, Philadelphia, shortly before the Declaration of Independence; that she said that General Washington made a redrawing of the design with his own hands after some suggestions made by her; and that this specimen flag and report were approved and adopted by Congress; and she received an unlimited order from the Committee to make flags for about fifty years, when my mother

succeeded her in the business, in which I
assisted. I believe the facts stated in the
foregoing article entitled, "The First
American Flag, and Who Made It," are
all strictly true.

Witness my hand at Philadelphia, the
twenty-seventh day of May, A.D., 1870.
S.B. Heldebrandt. Affirmed and sub-
scribed before Charles H. Evans, Notary
Public.

Betsy Ross' pioneer grandfather, Andrew Griscom, helped settle New Jersey in the days before
William Penn first came to America. A staunch
Quaker, Griscom was acquainted with Penn
and, in 1682, helped him found the city of Philadelphia. A carpenter, Griscom built the first four
brick houses there. His son, Samuel, pursued
that trade as well and, among other projects,
helped erect the belfry tower of the State House
(later renamed Independence Hall) in 1754.

Samuel Griscom married Rebecca James,
daughter of a wealthy importer. They had seventeen children, raising the nine who lived to
adulthood as devout members of the Society of
Friends. Their seventh daughter, Elizabeth, arrived on New Year's Day, 1752, the same year
that Benjamin Franklin flew his kite in her city
of birth. "Betsy" attended the Rebecca Jones
School for Quakers, which had been chartered

by William Penn. She showed a considerable talent for needlework and as a teenager apprenticed in an upholstery shop owned by William Webster.

A small crowd of young men usually waited for a glimpse of the lovely and vivacious girl after church on Sundays. They vied for her attention at youthful picnics and other outings too. Her parents were not pleased to learn, however, that their daughter's three primary suitors were not Quakers and warned her against involvement with any of them. Although John Claypoole and Joseph Ashburn were deterred by this injunction, John Ross had a clear advantage—he too worked for William Webster and saw Betsy at work all the time.

At twenty-one Betsy decided that although she loved her parents and the Society of Friends, she still wanted to marry John Ross. Though not a Quaker, he was a Christian—and his father was an Episcopal priest. In November 1773 the couple secretly rowed across the Delaware River in the dark so they could be married in New Jersey. When news of the elopement reached her parents, they disowned Betsy. In addition, the Quakers publicly excommunicated her. She and John were happy in spite of these humiliations, though, finding spiritual comfort at Christ Church. That church eventually became known as "the Patriots' Sanctuary" because of the zeal of its members for independence.

A year later they opened their own upholstery business at Arch Street below Third. By that time the rebellion against Great Britain swept the Rosses up in its swirling events. Ross' uncle started recruiting male Philadelphians for a militia, and John became a guard of the ammunition stores along the Delaware River near his home. On January 21, 1776 he died when the gunpowder he was protecting exploded, either accidentally or in a plot by British Loyalists. Betsy became a widow at twenty-four after just three years of marriage, a woman also cut off from her family because she had married outside the faith. One of her descendants wrote that during this period, Betsy Ross "sought comfort in the services at the old church to which she and her husband had been so devoted."[1]

Tradition says that about five months later in June, Betsy Ross received some distinguished visitors to the shop she had taken over completely after her spouse's death. George Washington, George Ross (her late husband's uncle) and the wealthy Philadelphia merchant Robert Morris asked her to make a flag for the country they were about to form. According to Betsy's daughter, Rachel Fletcher, George Washington was a regular customer and friend of her mother, who often had sewed for him. She said that although she had never made a flag, she would be willing to try.

General Washington showed her a rough sketch, and she suggested some changes as they conferred in her back parlor. Betsy saw some defects in proportion as well as in the arrangement and shape of the stars. She felt that the flag should be one-third longer than its width and that the haphazardly scattered stars should be in lines or a circle. In addition, the stars should be of five, not six, points.[2] The general made a rough pencil sketch of it, and Betsy spent the next few days sewing the flag in her back parlor.

When she showed it to the committee upon its completion, they ran it up the mast of a vessel at the nearby wharf. A few bystanders applauded. The men next took it to the State House where Congress approved the design. Although the committee had gone to other seamstresses, Betsy Ross' flag is the one they decided upon, and they gave her an order for as many as she could make. She continued making flags for the United States Government for the next fifty years.

This is the essence of the story told to Ross' grandson, William Canby, who in 1870 set out to prove his grandmother's account. Doubts had arisen as to whether she really had made the country's first flag, as well as the circumstances surrounding it. Critics of the Betsy Ross story argued that there were no official records of the transaction, and Canby had to concede that point. All he could find in the official record was from the June 14, 1777 Congressional Record: "Resolved,

That the Flag of the United States be thirteen Stripes alternate red and white, that the Union be thirteen Stars white in a blue field representing a new constellation."[3] There simply was no known contemporary written record of Betsy Ross' visit by the committee or her creation of the first flag.

Canby suspected that the lack of official evidence for Betsy's story was because the committee was acting in a certain amount of secrecy. Besides, at the time of the transaction, no one—including Betsy herself—may have realized its historial importance.

After interviewing his aunt, Clarissa Sidney Wilson, and two other of Betsy Ross' daughters, Canby presented a public paper at the Historical Society of Pennsylvania in 1870, which was later published in *Harper's Monthly*. Nothing has surfaced over the years to contradict the story. Nevertheless, three eminent historians asserted in 1930 that the first flag was designed by Judge Francis Hopkinson, although Betsy Ross sewed it.[4] Though these historians did not elaborate upon it, their statement does not contradict Betsy's story; in fact, it may only confirm her testimony. Hopkinson was a Philadelphian who attended Betsy Ross' church. It is possible that it was Hopkinson's pattern that the flag committee took to Betsy. And as one of her descendents maintains, "She never laid claim to designing the flag."[5] He also wrote:

Of the authenticity of the making of the first American flag, sometimes questioned, there is no real doubt through the nation at large. Betsy's high character, the truth-telling reputation of her Quaker family, and the statements of her daughters and grandchildren (some in affidavit form) to whom she often related the circumstances of the Washington interview support the belief that had not become a historic fact to millions of Americans.[6]

Author Ray Thompson remarked that Ross' daughters were raised strictly as God-fearing people and were not given to lying.[7] In addition, he maintains the legitimacy of the committee itself that visited the seamstress, since both Robert Morris and George Ross were members of the Navy Board and "it was important that the new Navy have some uniform emblem it could fly at sea."[8]

Betsy Ross was twenty-five when she sewed the country's first flag, and most of her life remained ahead of her. An ardent patriot for the American cause, she was outspoken with British soldiers who took over her house during their occupation of Philadelphia in 1777. They dubbed the fair-skinned, blue-eyed woman "the Little Rebel."[9] She also had a practical knowledge of science and medicine and frequently dispensed her homemade eye wash and other remedies to her friends. She ardently opposed the popular practice of bleeding sick people to rid them of "bad humors."

In 1777 Betsy Ross remarried. Her new husband, Joseph Ashburn, had been one of her most ardent suitors during her youth. Sadly, as with her marriage to John Ross, Betsy only had a few years with Ashburn. A soldier with the American forces, he was taken prisoner by the British and died in an English prison in early March 1782. For several long months Betsy went without news of him, fearing the worst but keeping busy with her business, her family (two daughters, born to the Ashburns in 1779 and 1781) and her service to the army (making quilts and blankets). She also left Christ Church and joined a new group, the Free Quakers. These were Friends who, unlike the original Quakers, supported the Revolution. They lent valuable support to Betsy during this personally trying time.

One of her husband's fellow prisoners, John Claypoole, was released in 1782 and, upon landing in Philadelphia, told Betsy that Ashburn had died. Ironically, Claypoole had also courted Betsy before her marriage to John Ross. The two found solace in each other and married on May 8, 1783. Their lives were full now with the upholstery business, five new daughters, Free Quaker meetings and Claypoole's job with the U.S. Customs House. He worked there until suffering a devastating stroke around 1800. He died seventeen years later at sixty-five, having been nursed all those years by his steadfast wife.

In 1827 Betsy retired from the shop, leaving it to one of her daughters. She went to live with another daughter in the Philadelphia suburb of Abington, where she remained vital and healthy. She continued to sew, but now it was for her family. Seven years later she moved back to Philadelphia to live with a third daughter. Betsy returned to the Free meeting but, sadly, the membership had dwindled to two—herself and the founder's father, John Price Wetherill. The others had returned to the original Quakers following the war that no longer divided them. After a few weeks of just the two of them being present, Wetherill remarked, "Widow Claypoole, there are but two of us remaining. It is not right that thee and I should continue to meet here alone."[10] They got up, Wetherill locked the door, and the Free Quakers were no more.

Betsy Claypoole went totally blind in 1835 but, remarkably, she continued to sew. At the age of eighty-four she died on January 30, 1836.

ℭndnotes

1. Parry, Edwin Satterthwaite. *Betsy Ross: Quaker Rebel* (Philadelphia: John C. Winston, 1930), p. 75.
2. Thompson, Ray. *Betsy Ross: Last of Philadelphia's Free Quakers* (Fort Washington, PA: Bicentennial Press, 1972), pp. 5-6.

3. Thompson, p. 8.
4. Morison, Samuel Eliot, et al. *The Growth of the American Republic* (New York: Oxford University Press, 1969), p. 221.
5. Parry, pp. xvi-xvii.
6. Parry, pp. xi-xii.
7. Thompson, p. 9.
8. Thompson, p. 9.
9. Thompson, p. 9.
10. Thompson, p. 68.

E LIZA
S HIRLEY

FACTS AT A GLANCE

**Founder of
The Salvation Army
in America**
Born October 9, 1862
Died September 18, 1932

Arriving in America at the age of
seventeen, with no official support from
the British Salvation Army, she re-
cruited her parents to help her begin
what has become one of the largest
evangelistic and charitable agencies in
the country.

E LIZA S HIRLEY

S eventeen-year-old Eliza Shirley had been working and praying for weeks about the opening of the first Salvation Army corps in the United States. It didn't bother her that the building they had rented for this purpose was a dilapidated old factory, or that she and her family were broke, or that no one knew who they were or seemed to care. She was bent on bringing people to Christ, and nothing was going to get in her way.

Her father, Amos, had plastered signs all over their Philadelphia neighborhood announcing the first meeting, set for Sunday, October 5, 1879. They read:

> Blood and Fire—The Salvation Army. Two Hallelujah Females will speak and sing for Jesus in the Old Chair Factory at

Sixth and Oxford Sts. Oct. 5, 1879—11
A.M., 3 P.M. & 8 P.M. All are invited.

Amos had struggled over what to call his
loved ones on the posters. He didn't like calling
his wife a "lassie," but "woman" hardly seemed
right either because Eliza was just a girl. He
couldn't believe how determined she was for
such a young person.

When October 5th arrived, Eliza donned a
plain dress and bonnet, her uniform from her
Christian Mission days back in England. She
and her parents held a street service on the
corner of Fourth and Oxford singing, "We are
bound for the land of the pure and holy." No
one seemed to notice. When they continued
having assemblies on subsequent days, people
did stop, but not to listen. Eliza usually got an
earful of insults, and sometimes rotten eggs.

These obscure and unimportant people, fa-
vored by nothing in this life, unknown and un-
supported even by their distant comrades,
possessed of nothing but a love for God and
their fellow sinners, held up the cross of Christ
over the manure and cobblestones of a Philadelphia gutter.[1]

Eliza Shirley was born to Amos and Annie
Shirley in Coventry, England in 1862. Her father was a minister in the Primitive Methodist

Church, and her earliest memories were of
praying at the family altar. During a Christian
Mission revival meeting, Eliza committed her
life to Christ when she was fifteen. The Mission, precursor to The Salvation Army, conducted evangelistic street meetings in which
Eliza quickly became active, in spite of her en-
dangerment by flying projectiles hurled by angry listeners.

William Booth, the Army's founder and first
general, appointed Eliza to the post of assistant evangelist at Bishop Auckland in northern
England, a coal mining region. She was sixteen. With her partner, Captain Annie Allsop,
Eliza thrived in her work among the miners
and was soon promoted to the rank of lieutenant. She gained the nickname "Gospel Trumpet."

Her father had come to America in the after-
math of the Civil War to work as a foreman at
Adams and Company, a silk mill in Philadelphia's Kensington section. Appalled by the working conditions and the ungodliness of the
laborers, Amos Shirley asked his wife and daughter if they couldn't expand the Salvation Army's
mission to include the United States. "This was a
great surprise," Eliza later wrote, "as I was nicely
established in my corps as Lieutenant, but the
more I prayed and meditated, the more convinced I was that it was of God."[2]

When Eliza shared this proposal with William
Booth, he tried to dissuade her. Matthew

10:37, he reminded her, said those who loved mothers and fathers more than Christ were not worthy of Him. The sixteen-year-old was daunted, but she could not give up her dream, even for General Booth. When he saw her determination, he told Eliza that he could offer no official backing because he was not prepared to begin a mission so far away. Nevertheless, "If you feel you must go, and you do start a work," he responded, "start it on Salvation Army principles. You may call it the Salvation Army, and if it is a success, write us, and we may see our way clear to take hold."[3] Booth's reticence stung Eliza, who felt "very small that I had aspired to such a proposition."[4] But it did not deter her.

Just before she left England, Eliza received a visit from Herbert Booth, the General's youngest son. He vainly urged the girl to reconsider her decision, but she had received a go-ahead from the Lord and would not be stopped. General Booth had told his son that if such happened, "tell her to be careful about the principles of the Army, to start right. She may call it the Salvation Army, and if it succeeds, report."[5]

The plucky seventeen-year-old sailed to the U.S. in 1879 with her mother and 100 song books donated by her English supervisor. They were reunited with Amos Shirley in March and immediately set out to find a place in which to conduct their meetings. Eliza recalled years later, "Rent of halls were beyond our reach, we had no money, no friends, no influences, nothing but the burning, unquenchable yearning to save the people."[6] Meanwhile, she became a popular speaker and singer at holiness and temperance meetings in Philadelphia.

In September Eliza became excited about a decrepit chair factory that was available for $300 a year. The one-story building had been used as a hospital during the Civil War and a stable since then. It lacked flooring and the unplastered walls were thick with filth. Several holes gaped in the roof.

"Eliza," her mother advised her worriedly, "people will never come to a place like this to worship." The teenager responded, "Mother, Jesus was born in a stable—surely this is good enough for the birthplace of the Salvation Army in America."[7] The owner of the building was startled at the prospect of renting it to two female preachers and asked to see Amos before he would consent. Mr. Shirley paid the man a month's rent in advance, drawn from his future salary.

That accomplished, the Shirleys worked to revitalize the old building. They covered the bare floor with sawdust and whitewashed the walls. Kerosene lamps cheered the cavernous place. Then they posted flyers around town announcing the October 5, 1879 opening of The Salvation Army.

With four days to go until the inaugural meeting, the Shirleys had everything they needed except, ironically, enough chairs. Their funds depleted, they took this latest of many material needs before God. He answered by sending a stranger to them who said, "The Lord told me to bring this to you. I do not know what you want it for, but here it is." His gift provided enough seating for 125 people.[8]

Their work appeared to be a dismal failure when night after night very few people ventured inside the building. Thousands started to attend their open air gatherings, if only to shout abuse at the Shirleys or pelt them with mud, sticks, stones, rotten eggs and vegetables.[9] When they asked for the mayor's protection, he said they were causing the problems and should stay off the streets.

One Sunday night, however, the tide turned in their favor. No one had shown up for the meeting, but a crowd gathered around a tar barrel someone had ignited. The Shirleys used the opportunity to invite people to their assembly. An infamous drunk known as "Reddie" asked if God could do anything with "a wretch like me." Amos Shirley promised that He could and asked him to follow his family to the building for the service. He did and the curious throng followed. Reddie went forward during the altar call and returned the following week neatly dressed and in his right mind. He was The Salvation Army's first American convert. His story created such interest that crowds flocked to the meetings, and many were won to

Christ. Soon the Shirleys ran out of room to accommodate all the people who swarmed to the services, and funds began to pour in.

During this time, Amos Shirley's boss told him he would have to leave his job if he continued with the Army. He chose the Army. While he and Annie ministered at the "Mother Corps," Eliza and one of the new female converts opened a second one in West Philadelphia. She wrote to General Booth in England asking him for an "officer" and "soldiers" to round out their staff. Impressed with the work the Shirleys had done, Booth sent Commissioner George Scott Railton and "six Halelujah [sic] Lassies" in March 1880. He also promoted Eliza to the rank of Captain. Within a month of Railton's arrival, New York and Newark, New Jersey had their own corps. In 1881 Annie Shirley opened another in Baltimore. William Booth visited Philadelphia in September 1886, deeply impressed with his band's persistence in the face of much opposition.

A few years later Eliza married Phillip Symmonds, who was also active in The Salvation Army. They had six daughters. Symmonds died while Eliza was in her forties. She held several important positions in both field work and at the Chicago headquarters, retiring in 1921 at the rank of commandant. On March 10, 1930 she took part in anniversary ceremonies at New York's Battery Park to commemorate George Scott Railton's arrival in America fifty years earlier. Eliza Shirley Symmonds died in Racine, Wisconsin on September 18, 1932.

ƐCndnotes

1. McKinley, Edward H. *Marching to Glory* (New York: Harper and Row, 1980), p. 7.
2. The Salvation Army Archives, National Headquarters, Alexandria, Virginia.
3. Archivies.
4. Archivies.
5. Wisbey, Herbert A. Jr. *Soldiers without Swords* (New York: Macmillan, 1955), p. 12.
6. Archives.
7. Archives.
8. Archives.
9. Wisbey, p. 14.

Harriet Beecher Stowe

Facts at a Glance

Author and Social Reformer
Born June 14, 1811
Died July 1, 1896

The author of over twenty books, she is best known for *Uncle Tom's Cabin*, the nation's first protest novel. This anti-slavery story helped popularize the abolitionist movement, which was a major cause of the Civil War.

HARRIET BEECHER STOWE

Harriet Beecher Stowe found it difficult to listen to the message on that cold, clear February morning in 1852. It wasn't that she disliked sermons. She had heard enough good ones in her life—those of her illustrious father, as well as those of her eight brothers, all ministers. This morning, though, it was as if every sermon she had ever listened to rushed together in a mighty, pounding chorus, rousing her to action.

Harriet felt physically and emotionally burdened by slavery. Worse, she couldn't figure out what to do to make things better, an impulse drilled in her by her father, Lyman Beecher. His dictum was, "If you see a wrong, right it."

But how? Harriet wasn't a pastor like her brothers. She had no pulpit from which to forward the cause of emancipation. Nor as a woman could she make public speeches.

On that frosty February Sunday, however, she found another way to speak against slavery. As the minister preached, Harriet suddenly felt herself caught up in a fantastic daydream. She pictured a vivid scene—a male slave was being brutally beaten to death by his master and two fiendish assistants.

Harriet could see their faces—the slave's frozen in pain, terror and helpless abasement, the master's and his henchmen's, fiery furnaces of hatred. The slave took on the appearance of her friend, Josiah Henson, a former slave who had fled the South and become a pastor. He was a gentle man who harbored no bitterness toward his oppressors, only Christian love and forgiveness, and a concern for his former master's eternal soul.

After the service ended, Harriet rushed home and quickly took off her overcoat. She sat at her desk while her family ate dinner in another room and hastily began writing down everything she had seen in her mind's eye. She later said it was as if the story had written itself.

The middle-aged woman quickly filled several pages, then she ran out of paper. Spotting some ordinary brown wrapping paper, Harriet hastily grabbed it and kept writing so the creative streak would not be broken. Her characters—a godly slave whom she called Uncle Tom, and a heathen slaveowner named Simon

Legree—sprang to life on the handwritten pages.

Little did she know that her scribblings, first organized as a magazine serial, eventually would become "America's first protest novel."[1] When *Uncle Tom's Cabin* was released, Harriet Beecher Stowe prayed that it would bring peace between the North and South. Instead it helped ignite a national conflagration that ended in the cinders of the Civil War. When President Abraham Lincoln met her in 1862, he is reported to have said, "So this is the little lady who made this big war."

Harriet Elizabeth Beecher was born in Litchfield, Connecticut in 1811, the daughter of Lyman and Roxanna (Foote) Beecher. A zealot for saving souls as well as society, Beecher was one of the nineteenth century's most celebrated ministers of what became known as "the social gospel." Harriet's mother was well-suited to his passion for social change; before their marriage, she had worked in a spinning mill in her native Connecticut. This was a new social experiment for young middle-class women. The mills roomed and boarded the young women, teaching them not only working skills, but how to behave in polite society.

Roxanna and Lyman Beecher had nine children, one of whom died in infancy. Mrs.

Beecher passed away when Harriet was just five. About a year later, her father married Harriet Porter, and together they had three more children. Beecher's goal for each of his sons was that they become ministers. He wanted them to spread the gospel throughout the country, a dream that came true. He hoped that his daughters would marry like-minded zealots and be proper wives and mothers.

As a child Harriet attended a school run by a woman named Sarah Pierce. Then she switched to her older sister Catherine's Hartford Female Seminary, begun after Catherine's fiancé died at sea. (At that time, *seminary* was a more generic term and referred not only to theological schools, but to secular schools as well.) When her older sister deemed her able, Harriet began to teach. She was barely sixteen.

At the seminary the young woman began to express herself by writing poetry, eventually filling several notebooks. This provided her with an outlet for her creativity as well as her emotions, which were considered taboo by her repressive family. (It is likely that the Beechers' fear of emotions was a result of their family's history; two of Lyman Beecher's sons committed suicide, and his daughter Isabella became involved in occult practices, particularly seances.)

Harriet hated teaching for her sister, longing instead to be a young and carefree girl.

The experience left her discouraged and depressed. Worse, Catherine also pushed her little sister into writing and publishing a
geography book that they could use at the
school. Although it was a successful project,
the more creatively inclined Harriet had not
enjoyed it. In addition, while Harriet had written the bulk of the text, Catherine had received most of the credit.

In 1832 Lyman Beecher founded Lane Theological Seminary in Cincinnati, Ohio with the
goal of training ministers who would convert
the West to Christianity. Most of his sizeable
family went with him. At twenty-two Harriet
hoped to escape what was for her the grind of
teaching. Unfortunately, Catherine started a
new school in Ohio and called upon her sister's
talents again.

Still, there were changes for the highly strung
Harriet. In Cincinnati she saw firsthand the effects of slavery on people's lives. While Ohio
was a free state, legalized slavery existed in
neighboring Kentucky. One day Harriet visited
the Reverend John Rankin, a neighboring minister who lived in Ripley along the Ohio River.
She asked him why he kept a lantern lit in one
of his windows, and the minister explained that
it was a signal for runaway slaves crossing over
from Kentucky. It meant that he was part of
the Underground Railroad, a network of people who provided refuge for blacks on their
journey northward to emancipation.

Rankin went on to tell a vivid story about a black woman who had come to the house early one spring after stumbling across ice floes on the Ohio River with her baby in her arms. The tale captivated Harriet so much that it became her most unforgettable scene from *Uncle Tom's Cabin*.

After Harriet married seminary professor Calvin E. Stowe and set up her own home, she discovered that a young black girl she had hired to work in the house was actually a runaway slave. When the girl's master came looking for her, Harriet smuggled the girl to a farm on the Underground Railroad twenty miles from Cincinnati. These incidents provided the backdrop for much of Harriet's writing.

About the same time, she and Calvin faced tremendous financial pressure. Lane Theological Seminary was barely limping along and at one point, the professors couldn't even draw their salaries. Harriet decided to supplement the family's income by writing both fiction and non-fiction for various magazines. Successful in that endeavor, Harriet published her first collection of stories, *The Mayflower*, in 1843.

Seven years later the Stowes moved to New England when Calvin accepted a faculty position at Maine's Bowdoin College. Harriet welcomed the switch, feeling much more at home in New England than she had in Ohio. Over the next two years, she went to work for *The National Era* magazine, writing a dramatic serial that left its readers spellbound. This was the story she first conceived in church on that cold February day, and this time she wasn't just writing to keep the family's finances afloat. Rather, Harriet's story about slave life was meant to rally Americans around the cause of emancipation. The petite woman's pen proved every bit as eloquent and biting as her brothers' sermons.

Harriet interviewed abolitionists, read much of their literature and drew from her own experiences in Ohio to write her stories. Before long the magazine's editor encouraged her to turn them into a novel, a possibility she had been entertaining herself. In 1852 *Uncle Tom's Cabin* or *Life among the Lowly* hit America's bookstores.

The novel became a national sensation, selling 300,000 copies in its first year. Just as Thomas Paine's *Common Sense* had moved the colonies toward independence on the eve of the American Revolution, *Uncle Tom's Cabin* solidified the North's position against slavery in the years leading to the Civil War.

Southern critics panned the novel, denouncing its author as coarse and revolting. One Southern man went as far as to send her a slave's ear in grisly protest. Many offered reasons why her account of slave life couldn't be true.

Another point of controversy was Harriet's portrayal of slaves as human beings who were in most ways just like whites. Many Americans—even among "enlightened" Northerners—thought blacks were less than human and definitely inferior to whites.

The following year Harriet traveled to England where the literary set embraced her enthusiastically. She also wrote *A Key to Uncle Tom's Cabin,* an apologetic book in which she supported the particulars of slave life as she had presented them in her blockbuster novel. Besides her other books, Harriet became a regular contributor to *The Atlantic Monthly* magazine and wrote several children's works and Christian tracts.

In November 1862, with the nation at war with itself, Harriet Beecher Stowe met President Lincoln at the White House. Her purpose was to urge him to sign an emancipation decree for the slaves. Two months later, Harriet and some family members attended a Boston Music Hall performance to celebrate the signing of Lincoln's decree. A man came onto the stage at one point announcing joyfully, "President Lincoln has just signed the Emancipation Proclamation!" Cheers, stomping and clapping exploded throughout the auditorium, producing a deafening din. Some people jumped onto their chairs and roared approval.

Then someone remembered that Harriet Beecher Stowe was present and began shouting, "Mrs. Stowe!" The crowd quickly caught on, taking up the chant, "Mrs. Stowe! Mrs.

Stowe! Mrs. Stowe!" At last she stood before them on a balcony of the music hall, leaning over the railing, waving and smiling.

Harriet's dream of emancipation, as envisioned in the preface to *Uncle Tom's Cabin*, had begun to come true:

> It is a comfort to hope, as so many of the world's sorrows and wrongs have, from age to age, been lived down, so a time shall come when sketches similar to these shall be valuable only as memorials of what has long ceased to be. . . . [A]nother and better day is dawning; every influence of literature, of poetry, and of art, in our times, is becoming more and more in unison with the great master chord of Christianity, "good-will to man."[2]

Other books by Harriet Beecher Stowe:

Sunny Memories of Foreign Lands (1854)
Geography for My Children (1855)
Dred: A Tale of the Great Dismal Swamp (1856)
Our Charley and What to Do with Him (1858)
The Minister's Wooing (1859)
The Pearl of Orr's Island (1862)
Agnes of Sorrento (1862)
The Ravages of the Carpet (1864)
Religious Poems (1867)
Queer Little People (1867)

Daisy's First Winter and Other Stories (1867)
The Chimney Corner (1868)
Oldtown Folks (1869)
The American Woman's Home (1869)
Little Pussy Willow (1870)
Pink and White Tyranny (1871)
My Wife and I or, Henry Henderson's History (1871)
Sam Lawson's Oldtown Fireside Stories (1872)
Palmetto Leaves (1873)
We and Our Neighbors (1875)
Poganuc People (1878)
A Dog's Mission (1881)
Life of Harriet Beecher Stowe (1889)
   (She assisted the author, her son Charles E. Stowe)

Endnotes

1. Fritz, Jean. *Harriet Beecher Stowe and the Beecher Preachers* (New York: G.P. Putnam's Sons, 1994), p. 70.
2. *Uncle Tom's Cabin* (New York: Signet Classic, 1981), pp. v-vi.

Bibliography

Garrity, John A. and McCaughey, Robert A. *The American Nation* (New York: Harper and Row, 1987).

Sojourner Truth

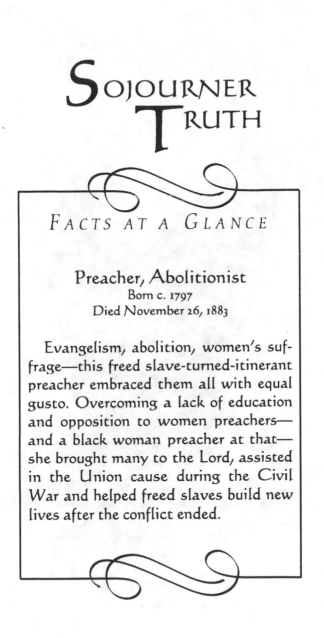

Facts at a Glance

Preacher, Abolitionist
Born c. 1797
Died November 26, 1883

Evangelism, abolition, women's suffrage—this freed slave-turned-itinerant
preacher embraced them all with equal
gusto. Overcoming a lack of education
and opposition to women preachers—
and a black woman preacher at that—
she brought many to the Lord, assisted
in the Union cause during the Civil
War and helped freed slaves build new
lives after the conflict ended.

SOJOURNER TRUTH

———

"Break up this here meeting, or we'll set fire to your tents!" shouted a large crowd of white men as Sojourner Truth, ex-slave and itinerant preacher, waited for her turn to speak at a Massachusetts camp meeting in 1844.

A white female minister was about to begin her message when the mob appeared and issued its threat. Sojourner watched in fear and trembling as the speaker stood wide-eyed and scared. Realizing that she was the only black person in the meeting, Sojourner hurried to a corner of a tent where she cringed behind a trunk. What might the mob of angry young men do if they got hold of her? Her cowardice was short-lived, however. Sojourner was a woman of faith and knew what she had to do.

She went outside and climbed to the top of a

hill overlooking the crowd. Gathering all her courage, knowing that Jesus was with her, she raised her voice in a powerful song:

> It was early in the morning,
> It was early in the morning,
> Just at the break of day,
> When He rose,
> When He rose,
> When He rose,
> And went to heaven on a cloud.

Both the rioters and the worshipers gazed incredulously at Sojourner as they took in her powerful, resolute voice. Yet the black woman's worst fears came true when the protestors suddenly dashed toward her. She saw that most of them were carrying sticks and clubs as they surrounded her on all sides.

When the men closed in, Sojourner stopped singing. Then she asked, "Why do you come about me with clubs and sticks? I am not doing harm to anyone."

To which several men replied, "We ain't goin' to hurt you, old woman. We just came to hear you sing!"[1]

Sojourner Truth entered the world as "Isabella" some time in the late 1790s, a slave with no freedom and no last name to call her own. Her home was Ulster County, New York, a state in which slavery was permitted until an emancipation act became law in 1827. Sojourner's mother, Elizabeth, who was called Mau Mau Bett, was the third wife of James Bomefree. Several of Sojourner's brothers and sisters were sold during her youth. She was, however, reunited with three sisters and one brother after each moved to New York City as adults.

One of Sojourner's earliest memories was of her master's death and the takeover of the property by his son, a man who sent his slaves to live in the small, drafty cellar of the main house. Mau Mau Bett considered them fortunate, however, saying that he was the kindest of the owner's sons. She also taught her children that there was a God in heaven who cared about them; they could always look to Him for help and guidance, and He would take care of them. Nevertheless, Bett frequently crooned mournful Psalms that pleaded, "How long, O Lord?"

During her childhood, Sojourner created a getaway for herself, an alcove fashioned from willow branches, where she got into the habit of praying aloud to God. She said that it helped her feel closer to Him. In addition, the child claimed that she and God conversed, although the nature of that discourse remains unclear. Did she actually hear God audibly, or were these strong impressions received in Sojourner's spirit?

When she was nine or ten, Sojourner's master died, and she was sold to a different man for

$100 and a flock of sheep. Although she was given plenty to eat, Sojourner was also whipped regularly and brutally, bearing lifelong scars from the mistreatment. When the situation got beyond her ability to endure, she prayed for deliverance. She also asked if her earthly father could help her. Upon their earlier master's death, James had been freed because he was too sick to go on working. Now he informed Sojourner about a tavern owner who might want her and said he would speak to the man about it. The tavern owner agreed to her father's request and bought Sojourner for $105.

She worked in both the tavern and on the general grounds until her new master came upon hard times. Then it was off to another owner, who bought the young woman for about $300.

During this phase of her life, Sojourner entered a marital partnership with "Bob," a slave from a neighboring farm. Slave marriages were not recognized by the law or binding to the master, who could do with the couple what he pleased. Sojourner's husband was beaten severely each time he tried to visit her, and the marriage eventually dissolved. They did, however, have one child, Diana.

Sojourner remarried around 1817. She and her new husband, Thomas, belonged to the same master and had had two earlier marriages. Each of them ended with the sale of those wives. Sojourner and Thomas had two boys and two girls.

When Sojourner's owner sold her son Peter across the state line, she determined to get the boy back. Her mistress thought this was ridiculous, although she knew her husband's action was illegal. She taunted Sojourner, "You don't have the money to get Peter back." "That's not a problem," the black woman replied, "God has plenty of it."

In the meantime, her master also broke faith with her on another issue. He had promised to free Sojourner in 1826, a year before the New York state emancipation act went into effect. When she pressed him on the issue, however, he refused to honor his word. Sojourner decided to escape with her infant. Reflecting on the incident in her later years, she said that God had led her every step toward freedom, right down to telling her which move to make next.

A couple called the Van Wagenens learned of her plight and decided to buy Sojourner's services for the rest of the year from her owner. They also went a step further in their assistance, helping her sue successfully for Peter's return.

It may have been their kindness that helped rid Sojourner of a raging bitterness toward whites. She had even wished for a time that God would kill them all. Sojourner began to love her oppressors, though, as the Lord gave her the ability to love them.

Shortly after the state's emancipation decree became law, Sojourner moved to New York City and worked as a domestic servant. She first joined the Methodist Church, then the African Methodist Episcopal Church, becoming active in volunteer social work. Elijah Pierson, a popular evangelist, noticed that Sojourner had a gift for public speaking and enlisted her services as a preacher. That continued until Pierson's involvement in a scandal surrounding his utopian community, Zion Hill. During the early to mid-nineteenth century, many experimental communes arose in New York State, where people tried to create a perfect society. Zion Hill was among them. It quickly became cultish, however, and the leaders constantly fought one another.

In 1843 Sojourner received God's call to adopt the name Sojourner, and to travel as an itinerant preacher. She later described this calling to Harriet Beecher Stowe, who recorded it for her illiterate friend:

My name was Isabella; but when I left the house of bondage, I left everything behind. I wa'n't goin' to keep nothin' of Egypt on me, an' so I went to the Lord an' asked him to give me a new name. And the Lord gave me Sojourner, because I was to travel up an' down the land, showin' the people their sins, an' bein' a sign unto them. Afterwards I told the Lord I wanted another name, 'cause everybody else had two names; and the Lord gave me Truth, because I was to declare the truth to the people.²

Her children became alarmed at the change in their mother, worried that she had lost her senses. Why would she take up itinerant preaching with its severe conditions? Where would Sojourner stay? By what means would she travel? Where would she get enough money to support herself and her family? How would she persuade the majority of people who believed that women should not speak in public? How would she persuade them as a *black* woman at that? Sojourner calmly assured them that she was doing God's work, and He would protect her like an umbrella protects one from the rain and the sun.

Sojourner Truth first ministered to communities in Long Island and Connecticut, traveling mostly on foot. She settled in Northampton, Massachusetts by year's end. Besides preaching salvation and God's "mystical love," she also became deeply involved in the abolitionist cause. In 1850 she journeyed to the West, speaking in Ohio, Indiana, Missouri and Kansas. She usually began her sermons, "Children, I talk to God and God talks to me!" She frequently broke into song during her speeches, lending an unmistakable air of drama to them.

She often spoke on the same platform as one of the nineteenth century's most eloquent orators, Frederick Douglass. In their most famous joint appearance, Douglass suggested that the answer to slavery was revolt. To which Sojourner responded, "Frederick, is God dead?"

She gained some financial support through Olive Gilbert's 1850 book, *The Narrative of Sojourner Truth*, in which famed abolitionist William Lloyd Garrison wrote the preface. After the Civil War, Harriet Beecher Stowe wrote a new introduction for the next edition, and it sold well.

During the Civil War, Sojourner Truth actively solicited supplies for volunteer black regiments. In October 1864 she had an audience with President Lincoln. She also served for a year as a counselor in the national Freedmen's Association, helping newly freed blacks to get established.

Following the war, she continued lecturing and preaching widely. In addition to evangelistic sermons, Sojourner promoted women's suffrage as well as a plan for a special western settlement for newly freed blacks. She retired to Battle Creek, Michigan in 1857 and died there in 1883.

Endnotes

1. Stetson, Erlene and David, Linda. *Glorying in Tribulation: The Lifework of Sojourner Truth* (East Lansing, MI: Michigan State University Press, 1994), pp. 95-96.
2. Ibid., pp. 87-88.

Harriet Tubman

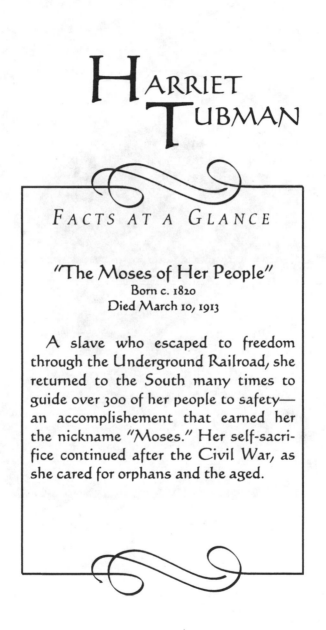

FACTS AT A GLANCE

"The Moses of Her People"
Born c. 1820
Died March 10, 1913

A slave who escaped to freedom through the Underground Railroad, she returned to the South many times to guide over 300 of her people to safety—an accomplishement that earned her the nickname "Moses." Her self-sacrifice continued after the Civil War, as she cared for orphans and the aged.

HARRIET TUBMAN

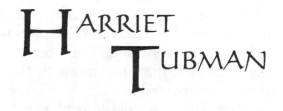

Eleven runaway slaves jumped at the sound of urgently barking dogs nearby. Their owners were hot on the trail, threatening to overtake them. Harriet Tubman's presence steadied the fugitives. At just five feet tall, this sturdy, strong-willed ex-slave hurried her frightened charges into a frigid stream. She knew from experience that even in daylight they would be safe because the dogs couldn't pick up their scent in the water. Her sharpened instincts proved her right again. When that danger died down, Harriet furtively led the runaway slaves to one of the farms along the Underground Railroad.

When the small group finally reached the appointed farmhouse, a stranger came to the door, eying Harriet warily. She asked for the man who had helped her before, only to learn that he had fled after the authorities had found him out. Harriet hurried back to the runaways, who anxiously waited for her in the woods. She knew that it would be only a matter of time before the new owner squealed on her.

They rushed ahead, feet aching and stomachs rumbling. All they had eaten for days were wild berries, corn, apples and an occasional fish when they had the time to catch them in the streams they passed.

Harriet Tubman encouraged the frightened runaways not to give up. She had been through hard journeys before and knew her way around fear and danger. They had total confidence in her. Wasn't she the Moses of her people, leading blacks to freedom as the Bible hero had led the Jews out of their Egyptian bondage centuries before?

Actually, one of the runaways wasn't so sure about her. When he stated his intention to go back, Harriet forbade it. Chances were good that he would be caught and forced to give up their position under duress. When the man insisted, Harriet resorted to the one argument she reserved for situations like this. She pulled a gun out of her coat and stated unequivocally, "Live North or die here." The man decided to live North.

One terrible day, however, it seemed they would never make it to that promised land. Harriet led them to a murky, foul-smelling swamp, explaining as they crept gingerly into the tall grasses that Underground Railroad workers often passed by there to offer help. Why the swamp? It was so awful that no one else would go near it.

As night fell, Harriet and her runaways shivered in the darkness. Suddenly they heard a man's voice, and their hearts pounded in fear and anticipation. The stranger muttered, "My wagon stands in the barnyard across the way." He also informed them that his horse was ready to go, and that there were plenty of food and blankets for everyone.

A little while later, Harriet ran a reconnaissance mission to the barn and found everything just as the man had said. When she returned to the others, she joyfully reported that the tide had turned, and they were on the way to freedom. "Praise God!" they cried.

Harriet Tubman entered the world as Araminta Greene some time around 1820; like most slaves, an exact record of her birth was not kept. She was born in a cabin on a Dorchester County, Maryland plantation to slaves known as Harriet and Ben Ross. Besides little Harriet, who took that name when she got older, there were six sons and another daughter.

She was trained from an early age to work as a maid, nurse, field hand, cook and woodcutter. She never learned to read or write, but

Harriet had an abundance of wisdom and common sense.

Her master Edward Brodas's financial situation caused him to sell some of his slaves when Harriet was about seven years old. Although she did not go on the auction block, Harriet was hired out to some of Brodas' neighbors for a few cents a week. One woman, known as "Miss Susan," employed Harriet's services to take care of her baby and do general cleaning. The situation did not go well, however. Every time the baby started to cry, for instance, Susan whipped Harriet severely, her rawhide switch making permanent scars on the young slave's neck.

One day Harriet was so hungry that she ate a piece of sugar without Susan's permission. The beating she received was so severe that Harriet ran away, taking refuge in a pigpen for five days where she competed with the animals for potato peelings. Deciding that beatings were better than starving, she returned to her employer. Susan was so irate with Harriet, however, that she immediately sent her back to Edward Brodas.

Another employer forced Harriet to work outside while she was sick with measles and unable to produce at his expected rate. In disgust he returned her to Brodas saying she wasn't worth the food she ate.

Harriet yearned for her freedom and constantly daydreamed about escaping. Her parents discouraged her, though, insisting that there was no way she could be successful at it. Instead Ben Ross urged his strong-willed little girl to trust her future to the Lord, that He would take care of her. It was a message she held close to her heart for her entire life.

By the time Harriet was eleven years old, she had become broad-shouldered and physically strong. She could plow and load wood like a man and enjoyed working outside because it made her feel like she was free. At night other slaves would gather in her parents' cabin and discuss an underground railway, a network of "station masters," "conductors" and "stations"—people and places—committed to help runaway slaves gain their freedom. "Conductors" were whites and blacks who went boldly into the South to help slaves escape. Harriet's parents disapproved of such talk, considering it dangerous foolishness.

When Harriet was thirteen and working in the fields one day, she saw a slave named Jim furtively head for the nearby village. The overseer took off after him, and Harriet decided to try to warn Jim that he was being followed. When the three of them ended up at a store in the village, the overseer asked Harriet to help him tie Jim up so the runaway could get a solid whipping. The teenager quietly shook her head.

Her refusal distracted the overseer, and Jim took the opportunity to flee from the store. The white man saw this happen and was so furious that he pitched a two-pound iron weight at Jim. It missed him, but caught Harriet solidly on the head. For weeks she hovered between life and death. After she made it past the initial crisis, Harriet was a little slow for awhile, and Edward Brodas tried unsuccessfully to sell her.

The tough-minded Harriet did recover, though not completely. Throughout the rest of her life she had a tendency to fall asleep suddenly, anytime and anywhere.

By the time Harriet had recovered enough to work again, Brodas had died, and a Dr. Thompson had taken over the plantation. He decided to hire Harriet out to various people, under the condition that she could keep what she earned after paying him a dollar per week. For a few years Harriet worked under that agreement for a builder named John Stewart. He treated his new acquisition as a trophy slave, regularly summoning her before his friends for demonstrations of her considerable physical strength. She did not appreciate being put on display like that.

Stewart's white friends weren't the only ones awed by Harriet. She also gained the attention—and affection—of a free black who worked for Stewart. John Tubman's parents were slaves whose master had freed them; therefore, their son had been born a free man.

John asked Harriet, now twenty-four, to marry him shortly after they met. Their union,

like those of most slaves, was not legally recognized. Slaves vowed to stay together until
death or distance parted them because their
masters had the right to sell them if he then
pleased.

Harriet confided to her new husband her lifelong yearning to be free. She expected John to
understand because he was free, but he did
not. Instead he discouraged her dreams. Harriet decided regretfully that when the time
came, she would just have to go north without
him.

Five years later, John Stewart made plans to
sell Harriet to a large cotton plantation in the
deep South. Little did he know that she had
her own plans. Harriet had long remembered
meeting a Quaker woman named Miss Parsons
from the nearby town, a woman who had
promised to help her if Harriet ever decided to
run away. One night before the dreaded auction, Harriet escaped, commending herself to
God's care.

A day later she found Miss Parsons, who remembered Harriet. First the Quaker fed her,
then she told Harriet where to go next along
the Underground Railroad. Harriet escaped to
Philadelphia via Camden, Middletown, New
Castle and Wilmington, Delaware, usually hid-
ing in cabins, attics and barns by day and moving by night on foot. She used the North Star
as her nighttime compass and consulted moss
on trees by day because it grew on their north

side. Finally she crossed into Pennsylvania, a free state where most people, particularly Quakers, were happy to assist fugitive slaves.

Of her first taste of freedom Harriet told a friend, "I looked at my hands to see if I was the same person, now I was free. There was such a glory over everything. The sun came like gold through the trees and over the fields, and I felt like I was in heaven."

Her only sadness was that her family was still living in slavery. She missed them terribly, vowing with God's help to bring them all safely to the North.

Harriet lived in Philadelphia for a year working as a domestic and making new friends. When she heard that her sister had escaped and made it as far as Baltimore, Harriet went after her, leading a daring rescue of her sister, brother-in-law and their two children. Even Philadelphia didn't seem safe once they got there, however. According to the Fugitive Slave Act of 1850, anyone harboring or helping a runaway slave—even in the North—had to turn that slave over to his master or face fines and possibly imprisonment.

This law, however, did not prevent slaves from seeking their freedom, or free men and women from helping them. Many runaways escaped to Canada to be on the safe side, Harriet Tubman among them. She made St. Catherine's, Ontario her home for the next five years, while helping other slaves escape.

In the fall of 1851 Harriet Tubman returned to Dorchester County, Maryland to find her husband. She learned, much to her disappointment, that he had remarried after her escape.

Her sadness did not send her into a deep depression, though. Instead Harriet grew more determined to rescue as many slaves as she could. In the years before the Civil War, she made nineteen forays into the South, freeing 300 slaves. She became a legendary figure whom blacks called "Moses." Like the Bible hero, she was leading her people to freedom. As much as she was awed and revered by blacks, she was hated and feared by slaveowners, who posted a $40,000 reward for her capture, dead or alive.

During one of her trips to the South, Harriet led three of her brothers to freedom. She had the opportunity to see her parents then, but her father refused to look at her. Instead he put a bandanna across his eyes so that when the master asked if Ben Ross had seen his children, he could say he had not. A few years later she rescued both her parents.

In 1857 the future Secretary of State William H. Seward set Harriet up in an Auburn, New York house. She spoke to many abolitionist groups to drum up support for her rescues, becoming acquainted with many of the era's celebrities, including Ralph Waldo Emerson. Even the radical abolitionist John Brown consulted her about his proposed raid through the

South. Referring to her as "General Harriet," he secured her promise of recruiting men for his effort.

When Brown led his famous attack on the federal arsenal at Harpers Ferry, Virginia, however, Harriet was so ill with one of her sleeping spells that she didn't even know where she was. Once she recovered, it was too late to send her volunteers. John Brown was dead. She revered the militant Brown for the rest of her life because of his efforts to end slavery.

From 1862 to 1865 Harriet served in the Union Army as a spy, scout, nurse and laundress in South Carolina, again putting her life on the line for her cause. After the war, with the Army owing her $1,800 for her services, Harriet returned to her New York home. Although she lived on very little money, Harriet began taking in aged blacks and orphans. To support herself, her parents and her guests, Harriet made speeches and sold vegetables and chickens door-to-door.

In 1869 Harriet Tubman married Civil War veteran Nelson Davis, who assisted her with her home for the destitute. He died in 1890, leaving her with an $8-dollar-a-month pension. The government finally gave her $20 per month for her war service. On this small amount of money, Harriet took care of her boarders and even supported two schools in the South for freedmen. Active in the African Methodist Episcopal Zion Church in Auburn,

Harriet never seemed able to give enough of herself or her money away.

In 1896 she purchased twenty-five acres next to her home with borrowed money and opened the John Brown Home for indigent blacks. It operated until a few years after her death on March 10, 1913. The Moses of her people had gone to her true Promised Land.

Bibliography

McGovern, Ann. *Wanted Dead or Alive: The True Story of Harriet Tubman* (New York: Scholastic, 1965).

Sterling, Philip and Logan, Rayford. *Four Took Freedom* (New York: Zenith Books, 1967).

MARTHA WASHINGTON

FACTS AT A GLANCE

America's First First Lady
Born June 2, 1731
Died May 22, 1802

A wealthy and genteel widow when she met and married George Washington, she shared the hardships of the winter encampment at Valley Forge to assist her husband and his men. As the wife of the nation's first President, she set precedents for the First Family and zealously guarded her husband's privacy, sometimes at the expense of public opinion.

MARTHA WASHINGTON

———⚬⚬⚬———

artha Washington was a no-nonsense person who disliked flashiness and social pretension. Her friend Abigail Adams once noted, "She is plain in her dress, but that plainness is the best of every art. . . . Her manners are modest and unassuming, dignified and feminine."[1] But though she might have dressed casually at times, Mrs. Washington was always neat and attractive. Nor could she stand sloppiness in anyone else, especially at the dinner table.

One day her granddaughter, Nelly Custis, and niece, Martha Dandridge, came to the evening meal looking less than presentable. The Washingtons kept silent about the breach of manners, but Martha seethed inwardly. Just as dinner ended, a carriage drew up to the house. The young women got all flustered when they noticed that its occupants were a male friend and some French officers.

"May we please be excused?" Nelly asked eagerly.

"Yes, we need to change our clothes and fix our hair," her niece chimed in. "We look awful!"

Mrs. Washington narrowed her eyes. "No," she said firmly. "Remain as you are. What is good enough for General Washington is good enough for any guest of his."[2]

———⊙⫘⊙———

Martha Dandridge, the oldest child of Frances (Jones) and Colonel John Dandridge, was born on June 21, 1731 in New Kent County, Virginia, near Williamsburg. Her mother educated Martha at home, with help from itinerant tutors. Like other wealthy young women, she learned needle arts and how to play the spinet (a now-obsolete version of the harpsichord). Martha, however, also enjoyed more robust pursuits, like horseback riding. She became an accomplished horsewoman. On one visit to her uncle's house, Martha trotted her horse, Fatima, up and down the staircase. Her aunt took her to task for this appalling behavior, but Martha's father laughed off the episode. "Let Patsy alone," he declared, using his daughter's nickname. "She's not harmed William's staircase. And, by heavens, how she can ride!"[3]

At fifteen Martha Dandridge "came out" in Virginia society, and two years later married a well-to-do planter named Daniel Parke Custis. He was thirteen years her senior. They lived on his Virginia estate—ironically named "White House"—where they had four children. Daniel Parke Custis, Jr. and Frances Parke Custis died as infants. In 1754 John Parke Custis (Jacky) was born, followed by Martha Parke Custis (Patsy) in 1756. Martha's husband died suddenly in 1757, possibly of a massive heart attack, leaving her one of Virginia's wealthiest women.

Less than a year later, she met a captivating officer at a mutual friend's Williamsburg home. The circumstances of Martha and George Washington's courtship are vague, but in the spring of 1758, she commissioned a seamstress to make "one Genteel suite of cloths for myself to be grave but not Extravagant (and) not to be mourning."[4]

Although Martha's father initially objected to the union because he didn't believe Washington was of a high enough social status, the couple married on January 6, 1759 at White House. In April Martha and her children moved to his home, Mount Vernon. For the next fifteen years the Washingtons lived happily at their Potomac River estate. They did not have any children by their marriage. Early each morning the family had a worship time, followed by music lessons for the children, and reading current newspapers. Washington was attentive to his new family, in addition to his oversight of the farm and duties in the Virginia state legislature.

Tragedy visited in the early 1770s. Patsy Custis had suffered from epilepsy since the age of six, and her condition progressively worsened through the years. That era's best treatments failed to cure her or relieve her seizures. At seventeen Patsy suffered her last convulsion and died at Mount Vernon. George Washington noted that her death "reduced my poor wife to the lowest ebb of misery."[5] In the ensuing weeks and months, her husband, her son and her faith sustained her.

Two years later George left Mount Vernon to participate in the Second Continental Congress in Philadelphia. There Congress appointed him the Continental Army's Commander-in-Chief. When Washington received his commission, he accepted graciously, true to his sense of duty. However, he wrote to his wife that he would "enjoy more real happiness in one month with you at home" than the glory of the highest post the military could offer.[6]

At the time there were some suspicions that Martha was a Tory—a loyalist to Great Britain—but the rumors proved silly and groundless. She was deeply devoted to the patriot cause, and her husband's role in it. Edmund Pendleton, who traveled to the Second Continental Congress with Washington, remarked:

She seemed ready to make any sacrifice, and was very cheerful, though I
know she felt very anxious. She talked like
a Spartan mother to her son on going to
battle. "I hope you will all stand firm—I
know George will," she said. . . . When
we set off in the morning, she stood in
the door and cheered us with good words.
"God be with you, gentlemen."[7]

The war began in earnest in 1775-76. Martha
spent each winter at her husband's encamp-
ments, making her first treks outside of Virginia. She would repair the men's clothes and
socks and visit the sick and wounded until the
spring battles commenced. Mrs. Washington
became a source of great cheer to her husband
and his men. She also tried to become an example for their wives. She told them, "Whilst
our husbands and brothers are examples of patriotism, we must be patterns of industry."[8] She
was especially encouraging to them during the
bitter winter of 1777-78 at Valley Forge. Upon
meeting her there, Baron von Steuben's aide-
de-camp remarked:

She reminded me of the Roman ma-
trons of whom I had read so much, I
thought that she well deserved to be the
companion and friend of the greatest
man of the age.[9]

She once shocked a group of society women with her homespun style during the Morristown, New Jersey encampment. While they arrived in all their finery, "Lady Washington," as they dubbed her, received them in a simple dress. As they talked, Martha knitted. At first the women were offended by her plain appearance, as well as her busy hands, but one of them later noted:

> She seems very wise in experience, kind-hearted and winning in all her ways. She talked much of the suffering of the poor soldiers, especially of the sick ones. Her heart seemed to be full of compassion for them.[10]

When the British surrendered at Yorktown, Virginia in 1781, another calamity struck Martha and her family. George took his stepson Jacky to the battle site, where the young man came down with a serious fever and died. He left behind a wife and four small children. Martha and George took in two of the children to ease their daughter-in-law's burden.

General Washington resigned his commission and returned to Mount Vernon, where he and Martha eagerly took up plantation life. This lasted only four years, however, when the Constitutional Convention met in Philadelphia. Washington presided over it, and it quickly became apparent to most of the delegates that he was the best choice to be the nation's President.

On April 30, 1789 he was inaugurated in New York City. Martha joined her husband shortly afterward and reluctantly began setting precedents for her new responsibilities as first lady. She was not overly fond of public life. She refused to be called "Lady" or "Marquise," among other suggested titles, preferring a simple, "Mrs. Washington." Martha hosted Friday evening open houses for prominent people, but she also set boundaries with them, zealously guarding her husband's well-being. At those nighttime functions, she would rise at 9 o'clock and announce, "The General always retires at nine, and I usually precede him."[11]

In spite of Martha's down-to-earth disposition, some detractors charged that she was creating a monarchical atmosphere. Attacks like these, as well as the loss of her privacy and constant demands on her time and attention, decreased the small amount of tolerance she already had for fame. In a letter to a friend she confided that being first lady had grown tiresome and that she had "long since placed all the prospects of my future worldly happiness in the still enjoyments of the fireside at Mount Vernon."[12]

George Washington officially retired from public service for the last time in March 1797, and John Adams became the nation's second president. General and Mrs. Washington reveled in their quieter life at Mount Vernon, in spite of a steady stream of well-wishers, friends and family.

On December 14, 1799 George Washington died at his estate. Two years later the Reverend Manasseh Cutler visited Martha Washington and made the following remarks:

> [S]he frequently spoke of the General with great affection, viewing herself as left alone, her life protracted, until she had become a stranger in the world. She repeatedly remarked the distinguished mercies heaven still bestowed upon her, for which she daily had cause for gratitude, but she longed for the time to follow her departed friend.[13]

She died five months later on May 22 and was buried next to her husband at Mount Vernon. An Alexandria newspaper obituary recorded, "She was the worthy partner of the worthiest of men."[14]

Endnotes

1. Boller, Paul F. Jr. *Presidential Wives* (New York: Oxford University Press, 1988), p. 6.
2. Ibid., p. 11.
3. Ibid., p. 8.
4. Fields, Joseph E. *Worthy Partner: The Papers of Martha Washington* (Westport, CT: Greenwood Press, 1994), p. xxi.

5. Ibid., xxii
6. Boller, p. 5.
7. Ibid.
8. Ibid.
9. Fields, p. xxiv.
10. Boller, p. 10.
11. Fields, p. xxvi.
12. Ibid.
13. Ibid.
14. Ibid.

Bibliography

Flexner, James Thomas. *Washington: The Indispensable Man* (New York: Signet, 1969).

LAURA INGALLS WILDER

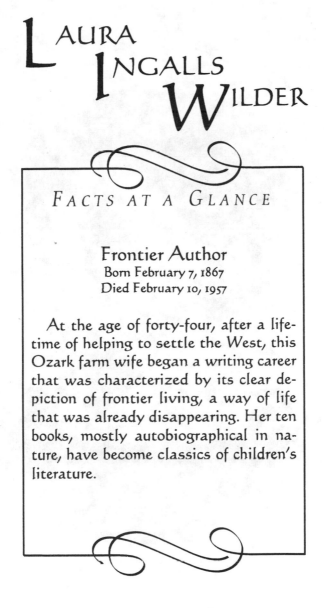

FACTS AT A GLANCE

Frontier Author
Born February 7, 1867
Died February 10, 1957

At the age of forty-four, after a lifetime of helping to settle the West, this Ozark farm wife began a writing career that was characterized by its clear depiction of frontier living, a way of life that was already disappearing. Her ten books, mostly autobiographical in nature, have become classics of children's literature.

Laura Ingalls Wilder

———⟨═∭═⟩———

Thirteen-year-old Laura Ingalls strained to read her school book in the half-hearted light of day. The blizzard of 1880-81 raged outside as if nature had pulled a shade on the sun.

"Ma, couldn't I please go out for a few minutes?" Laura begged. Bored and restless, she'd been cooped up for days. Although she read, sang and memorized Bible verses to pass the time, the teenager yearned to stretch her muscles and breathe fresh air.

"No one is going outside in this, young lady," Caroline Ingalls spoke sternly. She knew about people who, during other blizzards, had frozen to death between their barns and their cabins due to poor visibility.

Laura sighed. "May I at least have a little more kerosene for the lamp, then?"

"I'm sorry, Laura," her mother said gently. She hated to keep saying "no." "We have to conserve everything."

Charles Ingalls nodded. "We can't keep the snow off the tracks long enough for the trains to get through with supplies. I've also just heard that the stores in town are running out of everything. We have to make all our reserves last if . . ." He didn't add the last part of the sentence: "if we're going to survive." Everyone knew what he meant.

Fiendish blizzards lashed DeSmet in the Dakota Territory all winter long, creating snow drifts that rose to forty feet. No one went to school or church. The trains didn't make it in time to bring material Christmas cheer, but the tiny community quietly celebrated their vital faith in God, a faith that sustained them until May, when the first trains finally made it through.

Born in Pepin, Wisconsin, Laura Elizabeth Ingalls Wilder grew up with the American frontier in the final decades of the nineteenth century. Her parents, Charles and Caroline Ingalls, had come with their families from the east as children. They married in 1860, living in a log cabin village near Lake Pepin where Mary Amelia was born in 1865 and Laura Elizabeth on February 7, 1867.

According to the federal government's new Homestead Act, western settlers could earn 160 acres of land if they registered a claim for it and established a home and farm on it within five years. Weary of the constant clearing of trees and stones, Charles Ingalls took advantage of the Act, moving his family to Kansas in 1868. However, Ingalls didn't file a claim with the government land office and was unaware that he had settled on land belonging to the Osage Indians. He didn't realize his mistake until the tribe began debating war against all the farmers who were impinging upon their territory.

In 1870 the U.S. government paid the Osages $1.25 an acre for their land and relocated them in Oklahoma. The stately native Americans made a powerful impression on seven-year-old Laura as they journeyed past the Ingalls farm on their way to the new reservation. She, too, would spend her early years on the move in adventures that would become best-selling books later in her life.

Laura's family, which now included a baby, Carrie, moved again in 1871, this time back to their farm in Wisconsin. The man who had bought it from the Ingallses three years earlier decided not to keep it after all and had suspended his payments.

That spring six-year-old Mary Ingalls entered school, teaching Laura what she had learned each day when she came home. Laura developed a passion for words and books during those makeshift lessons and was encouraged by her parents, who often read aloud in the evenings. By that fall, Laura, not yet five, began going to school with Mary.

In February, 1874 the Ingalls went west again, this time to Walnut Grove, a three-year-old town on the Minnesota prairie. Life had been getting too "crowded" and predictable for Charles Ingalls in Wisconsin. Besides establishing a wheat farm, Charles and Caroline were among the organizers of the Union Congregational Church, serviced by a missionary pastor from Boston. In addition, a school quickly joined the tiny church as the bedrocks of community life.

Hardship fell upon the town in 1875 with a devastating incursion of grasshoppers. In 1876 there was a resurgence. The Ingallses had survived the earlier invasion, but this time Charles feared they wouldn't be so fortunate. He and his brood moved in temporarily with Caroline's sister in Minnesota; thirteen people lived under one very modest roof. Late that summer baby Charles Frederick, born the previous November, died.

That autumn the family embarked on yet another adventure when Ingalls entered the hotel business in Burr Oak, Iowa. After a year of living next to a rollicking saloon, they moved to a home on the outskirts of town. A fifth child, Grace Pearl, was born in 1877.

Life in an established town did not appeal to the footloose Charles. In the fall of 1877 the Ingallses headed back to Walnut Grove. Laura would say of that time, "Burr Oak seemed like a dream from which we had awakened."[1] She had moved seven times in her ten years.

Laura took her first paying job at age eleven, washing dishes, waiting tables and babysitting at the hotel in Walnut Grove. She earned fifty cents a week. During her free time, the tomboyish girl would find a quiet corner and pore over stacks of New York newspapers. Laura also loved reading the Bible so much that she memorized over 100 verses and large numbers of major texts. This resulted in her winning a competition one year at the Methodist Church.

At twelve Laura's faith in the God of those verses was tested. The first trial came when she went to care for an ailing neighbor away from home. Although Laura ached with homesickness, she took the job to contribute to the family's scanty income. During one especially lonely evening, she was praying through her tears when she suddenly sensed "a hovering Presence, a Power comforting and sustaining me."[2] She had a strong impression that God would always guide her through whatever she faced.

Shortly afterward, Mary went blind following a raging fever. Although the television series *Little House on the Prairie* portrayed her as sometimes bitter and resentful, in truth she took her affliction quietly and with an accepting spirit. Laura dutifully helped her sister with her studies, becoming "her eyes."

Within a year, Charles Ingalls accepted a new job from his sister, Docia, as the store manager at a railroad settlement in the Dakota Territory.

The Ingallses moved westward with the burgeoning railroad, at last settling in DeSmet, now part of South Dakota. The first church service in the new town was held in the Ingalls' home on February 29, 1880. Charles Ingalls went on to become Justice of the Peace, clerk, sheriff, street commissioner and a member of both the church and school boards.

In DeSmet Laura pursued her education with determination, undaunted by an acerbic schoolmarm. Eliza Jane Wilder had come out West with her two brothers. Although she and Laura clashed, the latter insisted on earning a teacher's certificate no matter what. That way Laura could help Mary, who was studying at the Iowa College for the Blind, where she had gone in 1881.

A Mr. Bouchie, who ran a school twelve miles south of DeSmet, was so impressed with Laura when they met that he offered her a teaching contract for that January and February. Although she was just fifteen, a year shy of the legal requirement, Laura took the job. She reveled in the teaching, not to mention the financial benefits—$20 a month.

The one negative was boarding at the Bouchie homestead, where the woman of the house was both depressed and hostile. Laura longed to go home on the weekends, but twelve miles was a great distance, especially in winter. Almanzo Wilder, her teacher's younger brother, came to her rescue. On Laura's first Friday at the school, Almanzo showed up after classes with a team of horses to take her back home for the weekend. This went on for the entire eight weeks of Laura's contract. Although she was grateful to Wilder for his assistance, she bluntly informed him that after February she did not want to see him romantically. He was, after all, ten years her senior.

In 1884 the industrious teenager took her second temporary teaching position, wrote prose and poetry and worked for a DeSmet dressmaker. Almanzo, whom she nicknamed "Manly," had won her heart by then, perhaps by his patient persistence. That summer he presented Laura with a pearl and garnet engagement ring. They were married on August 25, 1885 and soon embarked on the kind of itinerant lifestyle Laura had known as a child.

The Wilders' first home was on a farm two miles north of DeSmet. Since money was scarce, they worked side by side to avoid hiring outside help. They didn't work all the time, though. Laura and Almanzo loved morning horseback rides and church activities, too. On December 5, 1886 their first child, Rose, was born. Shortly afterward, the Wilders caught life-threatening diphtheria. Almanzo never fully recovered his once-robust constitution.

Three years later, Laura gave birth to a boy, but he lived only a few days. Weakened physically and emotionally, she spent most of the time in bed while three-year-old Rose did small chores around the house. That led to another crisis. As Rose fed hay sticks into the stove one day to heat the house, the bundle in her arms caught fire. By the time the incident ended, the Wilders' home and most of their possessions were gone. Laura and Almanzo found reason to rejoice, however; their precious daughter had not been hurt.

The Wilders decided to rebuild their lives back in Minnesota, but they lasted there just two years because the cold weather wasn't good for Almanzo. In 1891 they moved to Florida for his health. That venture, too, was short-lived. Laura suffered badly in the blistering heat, and they found the Floridians unfriendly to them because they were from up north.

A year later the Wilders hit the trail yet again, returning to South Dakota, where Almanzo worked at Charles Ingalls' store. He did woodworking and painting on the side as well, and Laura worked for a dressmaker. Their dream, however, was to take up farming in a more temperate region. This goal took the Wilders to southern Missouri in 1894. Laura sent her re-

flections back home to the newspaper editor,
and he published them in *The DeSmet News and
Leader.*

Laura and Almanzo bought a piece of land in
Missouri's Ozark Mountains and named it
Rocky Ridge Farm. It took them several years
to complete their home, finishing it in 1913
with the help of a small sum they inherited
from Almanzo's parents.

Laura began to distinguish herself in the raising of Leghorn hens, a venture that, though
seemingly unrelated to writing, launched her
on a journalistic career. On one occasion she
had been asked to give a talk about poultry,
but she sent a speech instead because she was
too busy. It so impressed the editor of *The Missouri Ruralist,* John Case, that he asked Laura
to start writing for the weekly. In February
1911, at the age of forty-four, Laura wrote her
first of many columns. In addition, she became
a freelancer for the *St. Louis Star Farmer,* the
St. Louis Post-Dispatch and the *Kansas City
Star.*

Laura continued writing and speaking about
rural life. She also organized several groups to
improve the lives of women living on isolated
farms. She helped establish libraries, arranged
social events and set up a farm loan association. However, her biggest successes were yet
to come.

Laura's daughter, Rose Wilder, had graduated from school and married Gillette Lane.

They moved to San Francisco, where she wrote for the *Bulletin*. A few years later they left for Kansas City where she joined the staff of the *Kansas City Post*. Their marriage eventually ended in divorce, and Rose started traveling throughout the world, establishing herself as a popular writer.

Rose's first book, *Henry Ford's Own Story*, appeared in 1918, followed by a novel, *Diverging Roads*. Encouraged by her daughter's successful career, Laura submitted a story to *McCall's* magazine. It was published in 1919. She and Rose then collaborated on two articles for *The Country Gentleman*.

In 1926 Rose went to Paris where she studied at the Sorbonne, then on to Albania until 1928. She returned to Rocky Ridge and, from the proceeds of a flourishing magazine serial, built a new home for her parents there. (They moved back to the original farmhouse in 1937.) Rose also settled on the farm, where she continued to write.

In 1930 Laura turned sixty-three. She began reflecting on the staggering changes she had witnessed in her lifetime, how she had gone from traveling by horse to traveling by Buick, how candles and kerosene had made way for electricity and the telegraph for the telephone. She especially considered wistfully how the American frontier had completely disappeared. She firmly believed that it should not, however, be forgotten.

That year she wrote her first book, a novel based on her childhood. Laura wanted American children growing up in the fast-paced age of technology to know their historical roots. In spite of Rose's considerable publishing connections, it took Laura a year to sell *Little House in the Big Woods* to Harper and Brothers. It was hugely successful.

That summer Laura and Almanzo drove their Buick back to DeSmet, South Dakota, retracing the route they had taken by wagon 37 years earlier. Although they enjoyed the trip, it did have its sad moments. Many members of Laura's family had died: Charles Ingalls in 1902, Caroline in 1924 and Mary in 1928. Carrie had moved away, and only Laura's youngest sister, Grace, still lived in the area. (Both Carrie and Grace passed away in the 1930s.)

Throughout the 1930s Laura's books enjoyed great success. Schools often used them to teach children about frontier life, but they also were popular because of the times in which she wrote. While Americans trudged through the bitter Depression years, Laura's books reassured them that faith and love were all that anyone truly needed.

The *Little House* books gained worldwide acclaim in the 1940s. After World War II, General Douglas MacArthur requested that they be translated into Japanese and German, so that the children of those nations could learn about American life.

On October 23, 1949 Almanzo Wilder died of a heart attack. He and Laura had been happily married for sixty-four years. Laura's writing, public appearances, family, friends and faith filled the remaining eight years of her life. Her goal was to live to ninety, as her husband had done. On February 10, 1957 Laura Ingalls Wilder passed away, three days after reaching her goal.

Books by Laura Ingalls Wilder:

Little House in the Big Woods (1932)
Farm Boy (1933)
Little House on the Prairie (1935)
On the Banks of Plum Creek (1937)
By the Shores of Silver Lake (1939)
The Long Winter (1940)
Little Town on the Prairie (1941)
These Happy Golden Years (1943)
The First Four Years (1971)
On the Way Home (1962)

Endnotes

1. Anderson, William. *Laura Ingalls Wilder: A Biography* (New York: Harper Trophy, 1992), p. 75.
2. Ibid., p. 83.

FRANCES WILLARD

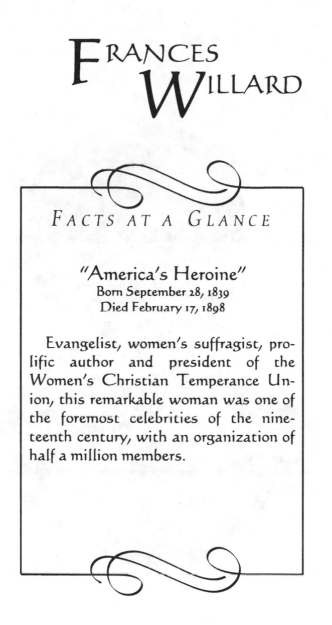

FACTS AT A GLANCE

"America's Heroine"
Born September 28, 1839
Died February 17, 1898

Evangelist, women's suffragist, prolific author and president of the
Women's Christian Temperance Union, this remarkable woman was one of
the foremost celebrities of the nineteenth century, with an organization of
half a million members.

FRANCES WILLARD

———⚬———

It was a biting cold night with a zero wind rushing across Lake Michigan. The street was mostly deserted but there was a sound of a distant singing of a hymn. . . . [The Rev. John B. Gough's] curiosity was roused. Around the corner, in the snow, under a flickering street lamp, knelt twenty-five or thirty women. Before them was a notorious saloon. They had been chanting the 146th Psalm.

As John came to pause beside a policeman a few feet away, one of the women began to pray.

"There they go again," groaned the officer. "McGuire had them enjoined from blocking his sidewalk yesterday and since dawn today they've knelt in the gutter. "Git 'em away from here or I gits your

271

star," says McGuire. "How can I git 'em
away?' says I. "They's ladies, every one of
'em. I can't lay hands on 'em like I could
some hussy from Water Street."

"The Woman's Crusade!" John ex-
claimed. "So it's reached Chicago! Who'd
have thought it! What can they hope to
do here?"

"They've closed fifteen saloons in a
week already; that's what they can do,"
replied the officer. Just then the door
swung open and a tall man in an apron
shouted, "Get the blank out of here, ye
blank . . ."

"Here, that won't do!" John said, as he
took a step forward. But the policeman
held him.

"They brought it on themselves. Let
themselves git out of it. Git back all of
ye," the officer said to the crowd of men
and boys now gathering.

A slender woman, slender even in the
plaid shawl wrapped over her cloak, lifted
her face and took up the prayer. John
gasped. It was Frances Willard!

The sweet clear voice rose above the
winter wind and silenced the barkeeper
and the crowd. John made his way
through the snow to kneel beside her. She
had turned the appeal to liquor dealers
into prayer. The bartender glared and
muttered to himself.

". . . O God, in the name of our deso-
late homes, blasted hopes, ruined lives,
for the honor of our community, for our
happiness, for the good name of our town
in the name of Jesus Christ sweating out
the passion of the cross, for the sake of
this soul which will be lost, make this
man cleanse himself from his heinous sin.
O God, open his ears that we may beg,
may implore him. . . .

"O God, pity women! Jesus Christ, help
the mothers of sons when their husbands
betray them. O God, pity women, help
them to end this curse! O, tender Christ,
torn in Thine consuming agony, give us of
Thy tomorrow and tomorrow, endless to-
morrows until this man's heart shall melt.
We are here, O dying, deathless Christ. . . ."

The bartender clapped his hands to his
head and uttered a howl, "Stop it! Stop it!
You can have the place, but I won't have
you praying my soul into hell!"

But she did not stop, not until whiskey
and beer ran like rain over the pavement
and into the gutter where she knelt.[1]

Charismatic Frances Elizabeth Caroline Willard spent most of her childhood on the Mid-
western frontier. Raised in a Christian home,
Frances had an older brother, Oliver, and a

younger sister, Mary. Her father, Josiah, was a businessman and farmer who also served in the Wisconsin legislature.

Although he frowned on displays of affection or emotion, Josiah Willard took an active part in his children's upbringing. He administered late-night feedings when they were babies and cooked when his wife was too busy. Frances grew up believing that shared domestic roles between men and women were the ideal. Mary Hill Willard, Frances' mother, was a teacher who home-schooled her children for most of their educations.

Frances became a tomboy, preferring to pursue carpentry and marksmanship with Oliver to sewing and cooking with Mary. At times this caused her anxiety; Frances often felt that she was strange in her interests and wished she could be more feminine like her sister. Her mother was unconcerned. Having Frances play with Oliver would one day make her son a more sensitive husband, she maintained.

Frances also had a keen interest in writing. She would get into her tree house and scribble in her journal or work at a novel. Some of her material ended up in small newspapers and farm journals later in her youth.

The young woman's formal education commenced in 1857 when she and Mary went to school at Milwaukee Normal Institute. Its founder was Catherine Beecher, sister of Harriet Beecher Stowe. Frances learned to cloak

her tomboyishness in the garb of unquestion-
able femininity.

Following one term at Beecher's school,
Frances entered the North Western Female College in Evanston, Illinois. She created quite a stir
on campus by telling people she wasn't sure
whether she was a Christian. The president, William P. Jones, was so concerned about her that
he had public prayers said for Frances. The feisty
young woman's doubts centered on whether
there was a God and whether the Bible was true.
Under duress from Jones, she went forward at a
school-wide revival in 1859. Shortly afterward
Frances wrote him a letter explaining that she
felt like a hypocrite.

That June she became ill with typhoid. During her illness, Frances said she "heard" two
voices—one encouraging her to commit her
heart to Christ, the other to hold out and not
give in to "weakness." She obeyed the first.

In January 1860 she joined the Methodist
Church. Although Frances remained a loyal
lifelong member, she fostered a nonsectarian
spirit toward all true Christians, which was not
popular in her day. She wrote:

> Before I ever declared myself deter-
> mined to live, being helped by God, a
> Christian life, I resolved to educate my-
> self in an unsectarian spirit. I honestly be-
> lieve that I regard all churches, the
> branches rather of the one Church, with

feelings of equal kindness and fellow-
ship.[2]

After finishing school, Frances Willard taught
for fifteen years. She earned a national reputation as a leader in women's education through
her natural public speaking skills and compelling
personality. She felt restless, though, because
education and public speaking seemed to be the
only fields open to her as a woman. Frances told
friends that had she been born a male, she would
have become a minister. Sometimes she worried
that she would never realize an intense ambition
to do something great with her life. Frances recorded in her journal:

> I used to think myself smart. I used to
> plan great things that I would do and be. I
> meant to be famous, never doubting that I
> had the power. But it is over. The mist has
> cleared away and I dream no longer,
> though I am only twenty-one. . . . I think
> myself not good, not gifted in any way. I
> cannot see why I should be loved. . . .
> Never before in all my life have I held
> myself at so cheap a rate. . . . It is a query
> with me, however, whether really I amount
> to so little as I think.[3]

In July 1861 she became engaged to a divin-
ity student named Charles Fowler, but broke
up with him in February. When evangelist
Dwight L. Moody asked her about the

breakup, Willard said that while Fowler had the temperament of Napoleon, hers was like Queen Elizabeth's.[4]

The same year she ended her engagement, her nineteen-year-old sister died of typhoid. Frances was devastated. Her first book, *Nineteen Beautiful Years*, paid tribute to Mary and came out in 1864.

In 1866 Frances came close to marriage again, but that relationship didn't work either. She remained single, deriving emotional support from, and lavishing her affections on, family and close friends.

Following a two-year world tour, Frances moved back to Illinois in 1870. She became president of Evanston College for Ladies the next year. A Methodist institution, the college was absorbed by Northwestern University in 1873 because of financial constraints. Frances became dean of women and professor of English and art at Northwestern, but her stay was short. Charles Fowler, her former fiancé, had become president of the school; the two clashed repeatedly, and Frances thought it best to resign. At the same time she became part of the popular temperance movement, a nationwide crusade to eliminate alcohol use and abuse.

Nineteenth-century Americans drank enormous amounts of alcohol, often beginning with hard cider at breakfast. Public drunkenness was widespread. With the advent of the machine age, there was a growing concern for on-the-job safety among male laborers, who were the heaviest of the drinkers.

Frances' energy and talents quickly won her the position of corresponding secretary for the national Women's Christian Temperance Union (WCTU). She had already assumed the presidency of the Chicago branch. Willard became a celebrated speaker for the WCTU, traveling around the nation with her message.

By 1876 Frances Willard headed the WCTU's publications committee. The national organization adopted her slogan, "For God and Home and Native Land." She also caught the attention of evangelist Dwight L. Moody, who was holding revivals in Chicago. In 1877 he asked her to become director of women's meetings, and she accepted.

Frances joined Moody's staff, eager to exercise her speaking gift for evangelistic purposes. Her association with Moody and considerable oratorical skills propelled her to national fame.

The two of them didn't always see eye-to-eye, though. While Moody shared her fervor for temperance, he believed that converting people would be, in the long run, more effective than the prohibition Frances advocated. It wasn't that issue, however, that compelled her to leave his group the following year. Although Moody was progressive in his attitude toward women in leadership positions, Frances balked over her primary use as a speaker at women's meetings. There is some debate over whether she left first or Moody let her go.

In 1878 she was elected president of the Illinois WCTU. During the next year, Frances boldly lobbied the Illinois legislature to allow women to vote on liquor trade issues. The "home protection" measure, as it was known, died in committee, but it did inspire similar activities in other states. It also created more publicity for Willard, and in 1879 she was elected president of the national WCTU, a position she held until her death.

A born "mover and shaker," Frances Willard linked many reform issues to temperance. She installed thirty-nine departments within her organization to meet specific goals, as well as to lobby and educate women about health and hygiene, labor legislation, prison reform, international peace, women's suffrage and other movements of the day. Through her efforts, such modern social institutions as public kindergartens, women's prisons and cooperation among Protestant churches all came about.

In addition, Willard promoted and established the National Council of Women, the International Council of Women, the Universal Peace Union and the General Federation of Women's Clubs. In 1891 the WCTU went international and Frances became president of that body. By the late 1870s, the WCTU's American membership numbered nearly 30,000.

Although she was sometimes too political for much of the WCTU's membership, Frances' undisputed femininity and her insistence that women had a special "sphere" of influence in the home retained a broad base of support for her. One of her major slogans was "Womanliness first—afterwards what you will."[5] She was convinced that by making women more active in public life, society would become purer.

Willard became America's chief spokesperson for temperance and the best-known Christian layperson in the country. No other woman of her time got as much attention in the press as she did. She went on relentless speaking tours; in 1883 she visited every state. Willard, in fact, lived on her speaking fees until the WCTU began paying her a regular salary in 1886. In addition, she wrote many magazine articles, mostly on temperance, and authored several books.

Not everything she did was well-received. During her later years, Frances Willard lived largely in England. There she became convinced that socialism was the proper form of government for Christians, that it promised everyone an equal share of the wealth. This position did not sit well with WCTU conservatives, but Frances never lost her widespread appeal. She knew how to play down the controversial issues while playing up ones that most women could rally around.

Another source of contention between her and the more evangelical members of the WCTU was her openness toward exploring other religious expressions. For example, a friend urged her to hear a popular spiritualist lecturer and read some of that movement's material. In the nineteenth century spiritualism was similar to the contemporary New Age movement with its emphasis on contacting "dead spirits" and trying to foretell the future. After her exposure to this, however, Willard came down firmly on the side of Christian orthodoxy. She wrote, "Oh Christ! All my quietness is through my belief in thee."[6]

In the late nineteenth century when Christianity pervaded American culture, Willard's appeal was huge. She was a national celebrity, and thousands of women followed her every move in the papers and magazines. Her organization boasted 10,000 branches and half a million members.

Miss Willard's life was cut short, though, after she developed a fatal form of anemia in February 1898. Falling in and out of sleep on the night of the 16th, she awakened one last time and whispered, "How beautiful to be with God."[7] She died at midnight, at the age of fifty-four.

Thousands paid tribute to this woman who had captured the imagination of an adoring public. Her funeral would have suited a queen. Flags hung at half-mast in Chicago and Washington, D.C. Seven ministers officiated at her funeral in New York City. Thousands of mourners filed past her casket to pay their last respects.

On the way to Chicago, the funeral train stopped briefly in Willard's birthplace—Churchville, New York—for another memorial. In Buffalo huge numbers of WCTU women streamed past the coffin wearing white ribbons for temperance and placing lilies at the bier.

In Evanston, the First Methodist Episcopal Church held final services for the woman who strove to improve people's lives through evangelism and temperance. Although she had not reached her goal of alcohol prohibition, Frances' devotion to the cause was unmatched and widely hailed. She had been "America's heroine." According to biographer Ruth Bordin, "No woman before or since was so clearly on the day of her death this country's most honored woman. Never before had an American woman evoked such an outpouring of reverence and affection."[8]

After Frances Willard died in 1898, the state of Illinois contributed a figure of her to the U.S. Capitol's Statuary Hall, making her the only woman to receive that high honor. Although her reputation suffered in the first part of the twentieth century because of the failure of prohibition, for a season Frances Willard was "the undisputed queen of American womanhood."[9]

CBooks by Frances Willard:
Nineteen Beautiful Years (1864)
Woman and Temperance (1883)
How to Win (1886)
Woman in the Pulpit (1889)
Glimpses of Fifty Years (1889)
Evanston: A Classic Town (1891)
A Great Mother (1894)
A Wheel within a Wheel: How I Learned to Ride the Bicycle (1895)
A Woman of the Century (1893)
(Edited with Mary A. Livermore)
Occupations for Women (1897)

Endnotes
1. Pamphlet, "A Woman of Prayer" (Evanston, IL: Signal Press, n.d.).
2. Bordin, Ruth. *Frances Willard: A Biography* (Chapel Hill, NC: University of North Carolina Press, 1986), p.29.
3. Ibid., p. 32.
4. Ibid., p. 88.
5. Ibid., p. 9.
6. Ibid., p. 157.
7. Ibid., p. 219.
8. Ibid., p. 4.
9. Ibid., p. 8.

J

3 5282 00448 5770